S0-BYE-297

leadership

BEYOND

EXCUSES

*The Courage
to hold the Rope*

DR. EUGENE G. WHITE

Leadership Beyond Excuses

Dr. Eugene G. White

ISBN 0-9748391-5-9

Power Publishing
7168 Zionsville Road
Indianapolis, IN 46268
(317) 347-1051

Copyright © 2005 by Power Publishing

All rights reserved. No part of this book may be reproduced without written permission from the publisher, except by a reviewer who may quote brief passages in a review; nor may any part of this book be reproduced, stored in a retrieval system or transmitted in any form or other without written permission from the publisher.

This book is manufactured in the United States of America.

Library of Congress Cataloging in Publication Data in Progress.

Published by Power Publishing
7168 Zionsville Road
Indianapolis, IN 46268
(317) 347-1051

Editor: Debbie DeWitt

DEDICATION

This book is dedicated to my Grandmother, Birda Mae Mitchell, because she loved me in a special way; to my mother, Elizabeth "White" Roseberry, because she did her very best to support and guide me in the right direction; and to my lovely wife, Jetties, because she has always been there for me in good times and hard times. These three great women have truly been the "wind beneath my wings."

A PERSONAL NOTE

A man is the sum of his experiences and those experiences are enriched by the people involved in them. I am the product of a single parent family from the segregated South. I am pleased and proud to say that I learned a great deal about leadership from people with little or no formal education. Ironically they wouldn't or didn't consider themselves leaders. However, they demonstrated outstanding people skills. They had the ability to analyze situations quickly and make good decisions. They knew how to involve others in decision making by talking to them and seeking their opinions.

One of the best communicators and interpersonal experts I have known was Bill Killings, a salesman and friend to all the people in the community. I learned great people skills from Bill.

Leadership was epitomized by my athletic coaches. They taught me the value of preparation, planning, execution, evaluation, fear and motivation. Leo Harrison, James Patrick, James Abrams, Duane Gordon and other coaches provided me with a foundation for leadership.

In my professional career I have been greatly influenced by strong leaders. Dr. H. Dean Evans, Dr. Jack Rigle, Lester Grile, Dr. Bill Anthis, Dr. Lowell Rose, Dr. Jack Snyder, Dr. Jay Thompson, Dr. Phil McDaniel, Dr. Ken Gose, Dr. Paul Houston, Mr. Bill Davis, Mr. Dick Horstmeyer, Mr. Max Lake, Mrs. Dorothy Turner, Mr. Lloyd Bowie, Dr. Patty Martone, Dr. E. Sharon Banks, Dr. Shirl Gilbert and Reverend Samuel Walker all have played major roles in my success.

I am blessed to have two wonderful children who are teachers. Kimberly and Reginald have made it easy to be parents for Jetties and me. They have made my life special. Reginald was even lucky enough to find a great wife named Elizabeth. She has added to our joy.

Yes, a man is the sum of his experiences and the right people create a synergy great enough to make a man's existence very special. I've been blessed.

ACKNOWLEDGEMENTS

Writing this book has been a very interesting endeavor. My wife has allowed me to take a disproportionate amount of time away from her and others to work on it. She was very supportive and understanding. I could not have written it without her.

My Executive Assistant, Cheryl Sutton, provided clerical and technical support for this project. She truly worked hard to help me complete this book. Tad Long provided support, technical assistance and helped to coordinate this project. I give a special "Thank You" to the editor for input and needed collaboration.

Finally, thanks to Dr. Al Long for giving me the opportunity and motivation to bring a concept from "just talk" to the reality of a book on leadership.

LEADERSHIP BEYOND EXCUSES:
The Courage To Hold The Rope

INTRODUCTION

<u>Leadership Beyond Excuses: The Courage To Hold The Rope</u> is a leadership book that seeks to identify excuses for leadership failures and refutes them by sharing practical successful ways to address the problems. It also uses a metaphorical perspective of leadership via a rope (vision/plan) analogy. The relationship between the leader's rope and the followers is the key piece of successful leadership.

The book reviews the challenge of leadership and how the leader's rope impacts the success and effectiveness of the leader. It looks closely at the eight common excuses for leadership failure and presents options to deal with the problems. The book does not pretend to have the answers to all leadership concerns, but it does present a unique way of looking at the tough task of leading people. Chapter one explores the Theories and Practices of Leaders. Chapter two defines, identifies and creates the "Rope of Leadership." Chapter three defines and refutes **EXCUSE #1: "If I had better followers, I would be a successful leader."** Chapter four refutes **EXCUSE #2 "If my followers would just follow my vision and plan, I would be a successful leader."** Chapter five explores and refutes **EXCUSE #3 "If I just did not have to deal with politics, I would be a successful leader."** Chapter six refutes **EXCUSE #4** "If I just had more money, I would be a successful leader." Chapter seven addresses **EXCUSE # 5 "If I just had more time, I would be a successful leader."** Chapter eight clarifies and refutes **EXCUSE #6 "If the system would work more smoothly, I would be a successful leader."** Chapter nine reviews and refutes EXCUSE #7 **"If only I didn't have so much competition, I could be a successful leader." Finally, Chapter 10 introduces and refutes EXCUSE #8"If only I didn't have to deal with change, I could become a successful leader."**

There are few, if any, acceptable excuses for leadership failure today. Demands for quality and accountability are at an all-time high. There is no cushion or room for excuses. Leadership at the highest corporate levels to the leadership involved with heading a family can all be described by the "Leader – the followers – and the rope" metaphor. This book relates to all levels of leadership and provides practical ways to become successful leaders.

There is no leader without followers and successful leadership demands that people be actively involved in the process. This book recognizes and identifies the role played by people in successful leadership. The rope metaphor ties it all together.

CONTENTS

CHAPTER ONE

EFFECTIVE LEADERSHIP

"Great leaders always work to build teamwork and cooperation. They never pretend to have all the answers. They know the best ideas and answers will come from the group or team."

Dr. Eugene G. White

Leadership Theories

I have spent many hours in study groups and in personal reflection about behavioral leadership attempting to answer the question, "Are leaders born or made?" Over the years I have studied leadership traits, practices and applications. I have appreciated the leadership traits of the "Effective Executive" by Peter F. Drucker; W. Edward Deming's ideas on systems and change; Paul Hersey and Kenneth H. Blanchard's "Management of Organizational Behavior"; Abraham Maslow's "Hierarchy of Needs"; Elton Mayo's studies on the human aspects of production; Amitai Etzini's discussion on power in leadership; and many others. I spent many hours in study groups and in personal reflections about behavioral leadership theory and absorbed the findings of Douglas McGregor's Theory X and Theory Y; and William G. Ouchi's Theory Z. In recent years I investigated the situational leadership theories and found valuable information in the works of Hugh J. Scott on superintendent leadership; Tom Peters passion for excellence; Ronald A. Heifetz's leadership without easy answers; Stephen R. Covey's habits of successful people; and Al Long's Theory "S" and his leadership tripod. Leaders are made, but some individuals are born with traits and characteristics ideal for good leadership.

It is a fact that I have been more than a casual observer of leadership ideas, theories, and practices. After years of study of successful leadership practice, I have come to the following conclusions about leadership:

In order for a leader to hold the rope of leadership which will be embraced and held by a group of followers, the leader must develop certain leadership qualities. The qualities of an effective leader are:

a.   *A leader must work well with other people.* Leadership is a people endeavor and people will make or break the leader. The success or failure of leadership is determined by the leader's ability to identify and influence people towards success.

b.   *A leader must be convincing.* The leader's passion must be supported by beliefs that the leader will have to sell to the followers. Leadership starts with believing and getting others to believe.

c.   *A leader must have the courage to challenge the status quo and institute change.* The leader must have the courage to break away from the status quo and "challenge the norm" or the way it has always been done.

d.   *A leader must be a good time manager.* The leader must be able to effectively use time "to be there," to lead.

It is important to note that all leaders are not created equally. Some come into leadership because of the job or position they hold. These positions create a certain amount of power. The President of the United States of America, the

Chief Justice of the United States Supreme Court, the Pope, The Secretary General of the United nations, etc. These are just a few examples of positions that place a person in a leadership role.

Many people transcend their position of leadership and rise to an even higher level. This level of leadership is created by the power or influence of the individual. This personal form of leadership is the most powerful kind. It means that people follow the leader because of what the leader personally brings to the situation not just because of the job or authority the leader holds in an organization or company.

Leadership through positional power could be successful and often effective, but leadership through personal power is stronger and it lasts longer. Few could question the fact that President John F. Kennedy was a leader and his leadership originated from the authority of the office he held. However, his leadership grew beyond his position and ultimately beyond his life time. His vision for the space program and placing a man on the moon demonstrated effective leadership. On the other hand, the dynamics of Dr. Martin Luther King, Jr.'s leadership grew out of his cause or purpose, his character and beliefs, his personal courage and commitment to the cause of civil rights and his magnificent oratorical skills which clearly communicated his message and extended his vision to others. President John F. Kennedy was the highest and most powerful public political and governmental leader in the World, but Dr. Martin Luther King, Jr.'s vision, mission, and actions made him a uniquely powerful leader of people.

There is another difference in positional authoritative leadership and personal leadership. It is the power to mandate or force people to act. Positional power mandates that the followers will hold the rope or else they will lose the job or experience a penalty. This could be a powerfully motivating influence, but it is only situational and belongs to the current person in the authoritative leadership position. This kind of leader fails to change the personal behavior of the followers because they do not own the rope. The positional leader owns the rope. The mission is seen as the leader's process or activity or the leader's change and when that leader leaves the followers often revert back to prior behaviors and practices.

A Leader Must Work Well With Other People

Leadership occurs because of the positive relationship between the leader and the followers. Leadership is a people business.

Jim Collins, co-author of the National bestseller Built to Last and student of enduring great companies conducted research to ascertain what separated good companies from great companies. He says in his book, Good to Great, that one has to get the right people on the bus and place them in the right seats before thinking about where the bus is going.[1] In other words, choosing the right people and putting them in the right places in the organization is more important than getting the organization moving. One of the primary indicators of a leader's success is the ability to put together a good leadership team with members who are able to embrace the leader's rope and hang on.

John Wooden is one of the greatest college basketball coaches in history. He won ten national championships with his UCLA Bruins Teams. Some critics questioned his greatness as a coach saying that the only reason he won so many games was because he was able to recruit the best high school All American basketball players. These critics failed to recognize that one fundamental part of great leadership is choosing the right people to be on the team. Selecting people who can hold the leader's rope of leadership and produce success cannot be underestimated.

A leader is no greater than the people who are willing to follow that leader. There simply is no leader without followers. Leaders motivate people to act and inspire people to follow.

There are numerous examples of both positive and negative leaders who motivated their followers to act. Mahatma Gandhi, Martin Luther King, Jr., Nelson Mandela, Geronimo, John F. Kennedy, Harriet Tubman, Vince Lombardi, Knute Rockne, Pat Head-Summit, Pastor T.D. Jakes, Reverend Billy Graham and others who have influenced or motivated followers to become better citizens or to make positive changes to society. However, there are also many examples of leaders who influence people to disrupt society, such as Al Capone, Adolf Hitler, Reverend Jim Jones, segregationist governors like George Wallace and Lester Maddox, a despotic ruler like Saddam Hussein, modern day gang leaders and hate group leaders (KKK, skin heads, neo-Nazis). These leaders have five basic things in common:

- They know and understand the people they want to lead
- They share some common connections with the people they lead, i.e. beliefs, fears, prejudices, education, religion or faith, etc.
- They can effectively communicate with the people they lead
- They can sell their vision or to the followers.
- They have the ability to share the rope or ownership with their followers.

The great difference in negative leadership and positive leadership is with the longevity of the leader's rope. Negative leaders' ropes are short and often die or end with the demise or death of the leader. Positive leaders' ropes are longer and frequently live on after they are gone. *Positive leadership builds legacy; negative leadership builds regret.* Throughout history the record clearly shows that leaders with positive messages of hope, service, justice, equality, love, freedom, fairness, inclusion, respect, peace, etc. create ropes of longevity and universal acceptance.

The Leader Must Be Convincing

To be an effective leader, one must be able to "close a sale." The leader has to sell the vision, cause, mission to the potential followers. This is often achieved by verbal and/or visual means. The frequently used verbal presentation has to be clearly communicated many times with persuasion, visuals, slogans, facts, figures and other supporting information. In some situations the leader's dominance (physically, financially, or politically) is great enough to hook the initial followers.

However, followers can easily identify leaders who are just going through the motions. The leader has to demonstrate the power of the leadership rope by symbolizing or being the rope. Vince Lombardi once said that, "Winning isn't everything it was the only thing." He trained and worked his football team in Green Bay like there was no way but winning. He refused to accept anything less. He came to symbolize winning. He was his rope in his approach to coaching and life. His players said he worked them all the same, "like dogs." He was an example of a winning leader not an excuse for failure. There was never any doubt what Lombardi believed and valued.

If a leader can not convey beliefs and values selling the rope will be impossible to do. Followers do not take the rope unless the leader is able to identify it for them and share its value with them. Leaders have to tell followers how they will benefit from holding onto a particular leadership rope. For example, followers need to know why it is important to meet the production projection for the week. They need to know what happens if the goal is met, or just as valuable, what happens if the goal is not met.

The leader must draw the picture or illustration for the followers to see. The followers must "buy" the rope's purpose or mission. The followers must accept the vision and hold onto it through good times and bad times. The leader has to find different ways to communicate or draw that picture for the followers. The leader can never assume the followers know what the leadership rope stands for until the leader communicates it clearly and often and models it himself/herself.

The leader must also communicate that the followers are important. The followers respond more productively when they know the leader cares about them. There is no leadership or victory without the followers. In order for the leader to sell the vision, the leader has to first sell the leader to the followers. The leader needs the followers' acceptance and respect. I tell teachers and administrators that "children don't care how much you know until they know how much you care." Followers, just like these children, need to know that their leaders care about them. Leaders should remember that followers want to be included, involved, cared about, and communicated with. This communication could be as simple as an e-mail, note, phone call, newsletter, personal greeting or meeting. All these activities demonstrate active caring. To say that the followers "know that I care" is an assumption too often made by leaders. The leader must actively demonstrate regard for the followers.

Communication is an essential key for keeping followers connected to the leadership rope. President John F. Kennedy's January 20, 1961 Inauguration speech was inspiring because it clearly stated his view for Americans and the world. It launched his "New Frontier" initiative. He told his followers, "…ask not what your country can do for you ask what you can do for your country. My fellow citizens of the world ask not what America will do for you but what together we can do for the freedom of man..."[2] His speech set a new tone for our country and our nation shared his vision for the future of the world. He said, "Let the word go forth from this time and place, to friend and foe alike, that the torch has been passed to a new generation of Americans born in this Century, tempered by war, disciplined by a hard and bitter peace, proud of our ancient heritage.... Let every nation know...that we shall pay any price, bear any burden, meet any hardship, support any friend, oppose any foe to assume the survival and success of liberty. This much we pledge and more."[3] President Kennedy painted a clear picture of his vision with his vivid words and forthright commitment to his leadership rope.

There is little doubt that his words would be the vision or rope of his presidency. He provided a message even more powerful in 1963 when he called for an end to segregation and discrimination against Negroes in the United States of America. He called for new civil rights legislation and laws to end our race problems. There was no doubt among his followers where he stood on this issue. His charisma, courage and intelligence elevated his leadership beyond the President's office or position to a personal form of leadership powerful enough to reach and move the masses.

Leading by Action

Some leaders are able to effectively communicate their vision more successfully through what they do even more than through what they say. Leaders like Nelson Mandela, Mother Theresa and Mahatma Gandhi are excellent examples of leading by action. It is very powerful to see leaders who are known by what they do or the courage they demonstrate. They not only communicate the vision, they become the vision.

This kind of leadership, where the leader is totally committed and involved, is a unique kind of leadership. The leader "sells out" to the vision. There is no safety net or cushion to fall back upon. There is nothing to protect the leader but the power of the vision and purpose.

This kind of leadership is necessary in education. In an era of high stakes testing and the increasing demands for public accountability, public K-12 education is now in a state of urgency. The average job life for an urban Superintendent is less than three years. Clearly this illustrates the crisis of leadership in these positions. Any leader willing to take this kind of challenge or opportunity has to be willing to "sell out" for the vision. With this kind of commitment level and Superintendent turn over, imagine how difficult it must be to get people in urban districts to buy into the vision of the new leader. How can we blame the employees because they have seen so many leaders or managers come and go? They have heard so many new visions. How can they believe that this time will be different? It is simply amazing how many of the teachers, parents and support staff in urban districts continue to generate hope for a better leader. Verbal communication alone will not convince these people. They seek and want to see action, commitment and change. Positional leadership will not be enough to lead this kind of school district.

There has to be a total commitment from a leader who leads by action.

A Leader Must Have The Courage To Challenge The Status Quo and Institute Change

No good book on leadership would be complete without looking at the relationship between managing and leading. Can a leader be effective without being a good manager? Must a good manager be a leader? It is ironic and appropriate that leadership appears in the dictionary alphabetically just before the "m" in manage. This is aligned with my personal view on the matter. Leadership sets the stage for management and management is a part of leadership. However, management controls and supervises the status quo or the "norm" and leadership extends beyond. Leadership redefines the boundaries of the norm. Leadership is dynamic. The good leaders ask the question, why not? Managers will focus on "how" but leaders must look beyond the details to the new way, the better way, and the not yet understood way. Managing is today and yesterday and leading is today and tomorrow.

It is important to understand the differences between managing and leading because leaders are frequently trapped in management's demands and practices that inhibit their ability to effectively lead. Today, leadership demands attention to results or outcomes. Educational leaders are accountable and responsible for improving the academic performance of all students and are commanded by law to "leave no child behind." The old ways of addressing instructional supervision will not meet the demands of the new mandates. Leaders must explore and find new ways to educate all the children. It is a tough challenge for managers, but it is a wonderful opportunity for leaders.

The great changes and progress achieved in science, business, medicine, education, engineering, agriculture, etc. have occurred because leaders broke away from the status quo and did something differently. Progress is imprisoned by the status quo. Leaders must continue to seek better ways to get the job done. Leaders do not lead by standing around; they have to take action. When great leaders take action for change they involve many others in the process. The key to effectively changing the status quo is in having others make it happen. Leaders need to share the ownership for change. Henry Ford did not make the Model "T" alone. He had to engage others in the manufacturing of a car that would forever change our means of personal transporation.

Taking the Next Step

Frequently the fear of failure prevents many leaders from making needed changes. The more successful the current operation, company, school district, church or campaign, etc. the more difficult is the decision to change. The old saying, "if it ain't broke don't fix it" is a powerful motivation for maintaining the status quo. Many good companies are not broke, but they will never get better without change. Jim Collins and his research team were correct when they said in their book, Good to Great, "Good is the enemy of great."[4] The practices, policies, rules, timelines, etc. achieved to create good companies probably will not make them great companies. We must find better ways to elevate our organizations to be more successful and effective. It does not take courage to make changes to failing organizations or companies with nowhere to go but up to improvement. However, it truly takes courage to take a successful or good company and make the changes needed to make it better. Leaders with the right vision, plan and the right people can break away from the status quo and make improvements. Leaders must work beyond the job description to step beyond the status quo.

There is really no such thing as a status quo for a leader. The leader is either moving forward or falling behind. The ability to change and adjust requires leadership beyond the status quo.

A Leader Must Be An Effective Time Manager and Be There To Lead

Leadership is a demanding endeavor. The leader is expected to provide the plan for others to follow. The leader must also take care of the vision through appropriate changes, initiatives, strategies, planning, coordination, best practices, data driven decision making and using "good old common sense." The leader cannot achieve success without the support and help of followers, but the whole process starts with the leader.

The leader has to have fuel to push forward and share the vision. The primary source of this energy is passion. Passion is more than the power a position brings. It is an energy source generated from beliefs, courage, will, determination, and the vision. *A leader should know that beliefs without passion are simply ideas.* Passion without beliefs is simply frustration. Beliefs are the foundation of who we are. They are the batteries that start our efforts. It is impossible to sustain the energy to do something in which one does not believe. To truly fuel the energy for leadership requires passion from the leader. The leader's passion can be contagious because others often gain their energy from the passion and energy of the leader. The defensive football player inspires great energy and passion with a hard hit or tackle. Knock-out hits really fire up the defensive unit. The contact motivates others to follow the example. Passion works like a knock-out hit in football. It fires up those who follow the leader. In leadership a knock-out hit might be a great speech or a great action or initiative. Passion can build synergy in a group of followers and fuel amazing achievement.

The leader needs passion to influence and motivate others. However, passion comes in different forms for different leaders. It is easy to recognize physical passion because the followers can see or hear it, but mental passion is even stronger for a leader. Mental passion is the complete belief in the vision. It can carry the leader beyond points of doubt, danger, and disappointments. *The mental passion for leading is stronger than the physical ability to persevere.* It is what the leader holds on to. It is what the leader sells to others or to the followers. I believe mental passion is rooted in caring. Someone once said that passion is love. I now understand that definition. Nelson Mandela's passion was so deep that the bars of prison could not defeat it. He spent 27 years in prison but he never lost his passion. There had to be others inside the prison and outside in the homelands who could hold on to their passion because of his example. His love and passion were great enough to see a multiracial democracy become a reality. As long as Mandela could communicate his passion to others, he was with them. They believed his vision and shared his passion. He was there with them even though he was physically imprisoned.

Mother Theresa did not raise her voice with passionate words or cheers. She was not desperately pleading for others to hear her. She demonstrated a quiet inner mental passion of force that could not be denied. She was driven by her strong sense of love and caring for others. Her vision, her mission, or her rope, was to love and care for people who needed medical and health care. She gave food to the hungry and shelter to the homeless. She spoke softly but her vision and actions were so strong that others had to respect her. Her passion was engaging and inspiring. She was there to lead and her action fired the flame of caring in people all over the world.

Remember, "People don't care how much you know until they know how much you care". People who follow leaders want to believe that the leader cares. It is wonderful for leaders to know leadership theory, behavioral psychology, and situational leadership strategies, but the followers really do not care about that when the battle is truly on the line. They simply want to know if the leader cares enough to hold on to that vision and be there for them. The leader demonstrates caring by sharing passion for the vision and concern for the followers. The leader can not build up brownie points for caring because the followers are operating with short term memories and the leader cashes out points faster than the points can be saved. It is always "now" for leadership; the momentum is always forward. There is no such thing as the status quo for a leader.

The leader will never be able to physically be present at all places and times for the followers. Therefore, the leader's vision must be clear enough for the followers to have no doubt as to what their roles are in holding the rope. The leader achieves this clear vision among the followers through effective communication and passionate repetition of the vision. The followers should always be able to answer the question: "why are we doing this?" Teachers and principals should know why children must learn. Players must know the game plan. Assembly line workers must know what the end product is. Why must I effectively do my job? Why must I care? Followers must also be able to answer the question. What is in this for me? What will happen if we fail? What is the meaning of this? Of course the leader must be able to answer these questions and connect the answers to the vision and plan. This is one of the leader's major responsibilities.

Leadership in Creating Leaders

Leadership will continue to be a challenging endeavor. However, the vision and the plan to achieve the goal combined with common sense and situational flexibility will ensure success and effectiveness. The global nature of business today requires a special kind of leader. The old days of top-down, dictatorial leadership are just about over. This model of one person with one vision, the answers, and the power is no longer the best model for success.

Leading by exercising flexibility, empathy, and focus on defined goals enables leaders to effectively work with all people. Leaders must see beyond the common obstructions of minor details or administrative bureaucracies. Leaders must now be more inclusive, dependent and collaborative. Leadership now is more situational and transformative. Leaders can be there for their followers by creating leaders among their followers.

The leader must continue to find ways to demonstrate that the followers are valued and appreciated. This could mean more employee recognitions, rewards, praise and personal communication.

The leader has to build connections with followers whenever possible. However, the main connection is always the vision and plan. Shared ownership and positive communication are essential in this connection. The leader has to convey to the followers that the leader will be there for them because everyone is important and needed to achieve the vision and the plan.

Range of Results in Leadership

Leadership results can be described in one of six basic outcomes: (1) Leadership that is successful and effective (2) Leadership that is successful and moderately effective (3) Leadership that is successful and Ineffective (4) Leadership that is unsuccessful and ineffective (5) Leadership that is unsuccessful and Effective, and (6) Leadership that is Unsuccessful and Moderately Effective.

Successful & Ineffective ⟶   ⟵ Unsuccessful & Effective

Successful & Moderately Effective **LEADERSHIP** Unsuccessful & Moderately Effective

Successful & Effective ⟶   ⟵ Unsuccessful & Ineffective

1.   Leadership that is successful and effective produces a result that is positive and progressive. A common example is the school principal who leads the school through a safe operational school year and has students successfully meet the academic standards and assessments at the 75% passing rate for the grade level. Just successfully completing the school year and taking care of all operational requirements is success, but the overall purpose of school is education not administrative operations. The academic achievement of the students is the effectiveness standard. Leadership can be successful without being effective.

2.   Leadership can be successful and moderately effective. The prior example with an academic passing rate of 60% could meet this example.

3.   Leadership can be successful and ineffective by successfully completing the academic year and having less than 35% of students meeting academic assessments

4.   In looking at leadership that is unsuccessful and

ineffective we see the complete failure of leadership. It is equivalent to an automaker who misses the production number of cars needed and the cars produced are ill equipped and poorly prepared for driving.

5. Leadership that is unsuccessful and moderately effective operates with poor or little leadership, but survives. This leadership outcome occurs when universities or colleges lose one or more president in rapid succession, but continue to operate in this leadership range.

6. Leadership that is unsuccessful and effective occurs when the followers get it done in spite of the poor leadership. This is commonly found in companies and organizations that fail to keep a chief operating officer or leader for any length of time, resulting in a revolving door of leaders. However, the workers continue to do their jobs and the company moves along.

A leader's success and/or effectiveness is determined by his/her influence on others. In today's business environment, leaders frequently do not have many second chances to do the job right.

Summary

The first part of this chapter has presented leadership

theories. In spite of all we know and understand about leadership, the greatest challenges to successful and effective leadership today are human excuses and dysfunctional organizations. This book will not trivialize the serious challenges faced by leaders. However, it will provide another way of viewing and attacking the problems. The challenge and opportunity of leadership is to find a new way, a new and better way to solve problems and operate at a higher level of service. The ultimate outcome of leadership is to provide a higher level of service to the organization, campaign, mission etc. and to the customers it serves.

Leadership is a people endeavor and people make the leader. The leader's passion must be supported by beliefs that he/she will have to sell to the followers. The leader's impact is defined by his/her influence on others. The great difference in negative leadership and positive leadership is with the length of the leader's rope. Negative leaders' ropes are short and often die or end with their demise or death. Positive leaders' ropes are longer and often live on after they are gone. Positive leadership builds legacy and negative leadership builds regret. The leader must have the courage to break away from the status quo and "challenge the norm" or the way it has always been done. The leader must be a good time manager in order to be present to accomplish the vision.

The results of leadership can be described in one of six basic outcomes: (1) Leadership that is successful and effective, (2) Leadership that is successful and moderately effective, (3) Leadership that is successful and ineffective, (4) Leadership that is unsuccessful and ineffective, (5) Leadership that is unsuccessful and moderately effective, and (6) Leadership that is unsuccessful and effective.

References:

1. Collins, J. (2001). Good to great. New York: Harper Collins.

2. Kennedy, J. F. (1961). Inauguration Speech.

3. Ibid.

4. Collins, J. (2001). Good to great. New York: Harper Collins.

CHAPTER TWO

THE ROPE OF LEADERSHIP

"Ropes could be connectors, protectors and projectors; ropes could be binders and confiners; ropes can be instruments of help or means to hurt. However, when a rope supports and pulls others forward it is one of the most effective ways to make progress."

Dr. Eugene G. White

THE COMPONENTS OF THE ROPE OF LEADERSHIP

Strands of The Leadership Rope

A rope is a very important help and support tool. People use rope for work and play. Ropes are used for climbing, fishing, rigging, hoisting, pulling, tying, sporting goods, construction, canvassing, manufacturing, shipping and mooring. Ropes are also used for aerospace applications, safety and rescue activities, construction and many more applications. It takes the right rope to meet the various needs of people. In all these activities the rope's main function is connection, service and support. It's essential for the user to know just how much weight a specific rope can support, and the breaking point of the rope. How much weight is too much for the rope to support?

In the same sense, the rope of leadership is also important to connect the followers and support the leadership task. The rope of leadership holds, pulls, ties, rescues, constructs, hoists, supports and serves the leader and the followers. It is essential for the leader to mold and choose the appropriate rope to successfully and effectively solve the challenges and meet the opportunities necessary for the leadership task at hand. The right rope will succeed and the wrong rope will break or fray under the pressures of leadership. The rope of leadership is forged by the strategy, the plan, the goal and vision of the leader and the followers. The rope starts with the leader, but the leader has to share ownership and buy-in with the followers. However it is the leader who is ultimately responsible for the rope.

A man made rope can be made with various materials. These materials range from conventional steel wire, cotton sash, nylon polypropylene, polyblend, polyester, and new synthetic fibers such as Kevlar, spectra vectran, dyneema and others. These new fibers are stronger than previously used materials, with higher heat resistance, abrasion resistance; flex fatigue resistance. They are more colorful and adaptable to various usages. The rope's diameter varies. It could be 3-strand, eight braided, solid braid sash cord, twisted rope, or have a parallel core. Ropes are manufactured from the core yarns to the cover. There is more to a rope than one can easily see just as there is much more to leadership.

The rope of leadership is created or manufactured through the leader's experiences and knowledge and the follower's willingness to accept the leader's vision and leadership directions. The leader must clearly understand the plan, strategy or vision of the leadership task because the rope will be just as strong as the leader makes it. The rope of leadership is created from the following characteristics: Beliefs, Values, Passion, Purpose, Courage and Vision. Together these characteristics determine success or failure.

The materials needed to manufacture a man-made rope may vary with innovative technology or new fibers, but the characteristics for the rope of leadership are solid and time tested. The weight of the load could be heavy, but the solid rope created by the leader will not break. The pull of tough decisions may create tremendous stress and pressure, but the endurance and stability of the rope of effective leadership will not be compromised.

Beliefs

One's beliefs are the foundation of who one is and the first strand in the rope of leadership. Our acceptance of ideas, acts, words, statements, with or without evidence of their validity or truth, make up our beliefs. Beliefs are not all reasonable or logical. Experts in child development suggest that people are heavily shaped by situations and activities they are exposed to in the first ten to fifteen years of life. These activities form the foundation of one's belief system. Other people strongly influence our beliefs and in today's society, even the various media provide unlimited sources of information that influence beliefs.

One example of an influence which might greatly affect one's belief system would be the spiritual leaders one is exposed to in the early years of life. Many important leaders have been shaped by the spiritual or religious messages they heard as children. An important aspect of the rope of leadership which each leader brings to the leadership task is a religious or spiritual belief system. It is the part of a belief system which allows the leader to recognize there is a force "bigger" than self which shapes events.

Consider the example of the leader who attends a certain Baptist church as a child and young man. This leader considers the pastor of this church his first example of effective leadership. This pastor taught the congregation the scriptural precepts of the Bible and the gospel message and convinced his listeners to accept these principles as the basis for their own belief systems. While the young man did not understand all the dynamics of his pastor's leadership, it was obvious to him that the members of this church understood and accepted the pastor's message, and that the pastor's message influenced their beliefs. Those who remained in this congregation continued to support their pastor because they agreed with the message and the pastor's leadership strengthened their organization. The pastor's belief in the gospel he was preaching was a major component of this rope of leadership and the source of his knowledge. His followers bought into the pastor's rope of leadership and accepted the beliefs he preached.

Another important influence on one's belief system is the political leaders one hears. A young woman studying leadership principles was impacted and influenced by President John F. Kennedy's leadership. The television debates between Kennedy and Nixon captured this young woman's attention when she watched them on television. What she found captivating about Kennedy was that to her, he sounded better and looked more like he belonged on television or in the White House than did his adversary. This woman was impressed by his visual image, physical appearance and rhetorical style. In other words, Kennedy had the qualities she believed a leader should possess: the physical appearance and presence of a leader. Her belief that a President should "look a certain way" influenced her choice of the leadership candidate she preferred. It was not until much later that she was impacted by the verbal message he espoused. A strong leadership presence caused the American people to vote for John F. Kennedy to be their President. His presidential appearance was a major part of his leadership rope.

Dr. Martin Luther King, Jr. is another example of influential leadership of the 20th century. He was a civil rights leader with a message of civil rights and justice which resonated with an entire generation of followers. He was also a Baptist preacher and his rope of leadership message was a three-strand rope of religion, liberty and justice. Many people's basic beliefs about civil rights, voting and justice were shaped by the leadership rope of Dr. King's message. His courage in the face of death threats and the bombing of his home are convincing arguments of how strong were those strands of his leadership rope.

Many people held that rope with Dr. King and part of them are still holding that rope today. Each rope of leadership that they forge contains the beliefs instilled by Dr. King. King said in many speeches "If a man hasn't found something he is willing to die for, he isn't fit to live."[1] Strong words provided a strong strand in his leadership rope and helped to shape the beliefs of his followers.

Beliefs form the substance of our action. An old saying says, "You must believe it to achieve it!" Beliefs provide the leader with a common ground with his/her followers. In the field of education, for example, if the leader believes that all children can learn, that belief should be strong enough to direct his/her actions to ensure that all the children learn. Without beliefs there is nothing to ground or center the leader.   Peter Marshall, the late chaplain to the United States Senate, once prayed these words on behalf of the nation's leaders, "Give us clear vision, O God, that we may know where to stand and what to stand for because unless we stand for something, we shall fall for anything."

Beliefs gauge the essence of the leader's character. Tug McGraw died in 2003, but once he was a famous New York Mets pitcher who popularized the phrase "You gotta believe!" In order to win, you gotta believe! In order to lead, you gotta believe! To paraphrase his message in the context of leadership one might say, In order to lead, you gotta believe!

The leadership rope is constructed by starting with a strong belief strand. This is the fiber that endures the heavy lifting and the stress of effective leadership.

Values:

Beliefs create a core of assets called values. Values are what we truly treasure and care about and these values form the next strand of the leader's rope of leadership. I frequently tell school administrators and teachers that "children don't care how much you know until they know how much you care." What one cares deeply about becomes something one values. These values represents tremendous importance to ones leadership rope.

The corporate community is still trying to recover

from the image of greed demonstrated by executives at Enron, Adelphia, Tyco, Arthur Anderson and others. The leaders of these companies were so consumed by their own value of having money, that they disregarded the financial needs of their followers, employees and investors. Their greed demonstrated that they valued money over doing the right things for people. Their selfish defined their values.

If the leader values the production of a product over the well being of employees the leader's decisions, actions and words will demonstrate that fact. If the leader values the approval of the followers over the achievement of the goal, the leader's actions will follow that value. Values are important in the relationships among people and between the leader and the followers. Values define and unite or divide people.

In the arena of education, for example, school principals and teachers work most effectively when they all value and agree about what constitutes quality education for children. This value enable them to speak a common language and provides a common understanding that guides and focuses their efforts.

Values are so fundamental for leaders that many frequently share their values with followers very early in the relationship. The leadership rope's value strand is very powerful. The values of some of the great leaders of the past are easily identified in how their followers shared those values. For example, Nelson Mandela's value of liberty and justice for his people was visible to others who also valued and loved liberty and justice and bonded with Mandela.

Athletic coaches build programs based upon operational

values shared with and accepted by their followers. Many coaches of high school and college sports the coaches clearly and dynamically communicate their beliefs and values to their teams in non-negotiable terms. Their message is often that "it has to be their way or no way." They frequently write out these values and give them to their teams because they want no misunderstandings. Some common values held and communicated by successful coaches are: Honesty is the best policy; I will not work with anyone I can't believe; Work hard!; Success is 10% inspiration and 90% perspiration!; Be prompt and always on time because the early bird gets the worm; There is no "I" in Team!; No one is more important than the team; There is no substitute for preparation, always be prepared. All these sayings are just words unless the coach models and espouses these values and beliefs.

These values, clearly articulated and communicated allow teams to better understand how they can please and play for their coaches. The values of the coaches, like any other leaders, are a fundamental part of their leadership rope.

Passion:

Passion is another important strand in the leadership rope because it provides the energy and fuel that drives the leader and the followers to achieve their goal. Passion is generated from the leader's strong beliefs and values. It is this passion for action which causes the leader and the followers to hold the rope.

Passion is a dynamic motivation to keep going through

the difficulties. People with passion do not burn out, they keep going. Their passion for achieving the goal transcends their "self" interests. Some examples of how passion pushes people beyond their limits of safety and self would be the Japanese "Kamikaze" pilots of World War II. These pilots were so passionate about their beliefs and values, their "honor" and "victory", that they flew suicidal missions and crashed their airplanes into the ships of the United States.

Today in the Middle East, people in Israel and Palestine are so passionate about their beliefs and rights to certain land holdings that they give up their lives in suicidal bombings of buses, public places. There are Islamic militants in Afghanistan who are willing to give up their lives in suicide bombings because of their belief in a fundamentalist Jihad or Holy war for Allah. The war in Iraq is fueled by the clash of beliefs between Democracy and tribal dictators. Passion is powerful! Maybe not always beneficial to all, but still powerful. When beliefs and values encounter challenges, passion can motivate people to hold on to whatever rope of leadership resonates with these belief systems, even to committing the ultimate act of sacrifice – giving one's life. These examples are not positive ones, but they illustrate the power generated when strong beliefs and values meet strong opposition.

A positive example of this passion is demonstrated by the preparation, dedication and hard work of athletes training for the Olympic Games. Their passion for success, glory and victory drives their work ethic. This is the ultimate example of holding onto the rope of leadership.

It is the responsibility of the leader to ignite this passion for causes which uplift followers and benefit the majority of people. Such is the drive for democracy in Iraq or Afghanistan.

In the realm of public education, as well as in other areas of employment, each year there are a few employees who retire, quit or change jobs because they are "burned out." These people have lost their passion to do the job. When an employee loses the passion for the job, it is part of the responsibility of the leader to encourage these followers to resign their positions or rekindle the fire that has been extinguished. Without the fuel and energy of passion, no one can work effectively with children and other employees. When a worker has passion for the job, every day is a good day. Getting up and preparing for work is a joy not a job. Passion colors one's view and mind-set about work and about life.

The leader needs to weave the strand of passion into his/her rope of leadership. An example of passion for success can be seen in the first generation immigrants to the United States. Their passion became a will to succeed in their new homeland. They developed and displayed a tremendous work ethic – willing to work long hours in excruciating conditions to provide for their families and create new lives for themselves.

There are numerous examples of how passion has shaped the history of our country. The United States of America has fought in two World Wars, a Revolutionary War, and a Civil War, wars in Viet Nam, Desert Storm, Korea, and Iraq because of its belief in the basic freedoms of people and its value for Democracy. In wars, the passion of our beliefs and values drives us to take the necessary means to secure victory.

In the Jewish Holocaust, passionate leaders led followers to survive and endure the ghettoes, concentration camps, mass killings or genocide of the European Jews by the German Nazis. In the Civil Rights campaigns of the late fifties and sixties, the beliefs and values of passionate leaders led minority followers to face vicious dogs, high-pressured water hoses, unsafe jail cells, bombings, assassinations and lynchings to achieve the ultimate victory of equality and justice. No one, especially a leader, can afford to underestimate the power of passion. Passion is a key strand in the rope of leadership.

Purpose:

The strand of purpose makes the leadership rope strong because it pulls together the strands of beliefs, values, and passion. Purpose organizes the other strands for success. In order to create the strand of purpose, the leader must seek to answer the questions about what the leadership task is accomplishing and why the accomplishment of this task is significant.

Beliefs are not productive in isolation and values lose their meaning when they fail to motivate us to help others. *Passion without purpose is unidentifiable and masquerades as insanity.* Purpose unites and creates a special synergy among beliefs, values and passion. In athletics, the purpose of competing in a sport is clearly winning. Coaches teach teamwork, sportsmanship, discipline, but without victory the purpose is incomplete.

If the purpose or goal is to find the cure for the common cold and during our research we find medications to make colds less painful, or reduces the duration of a cold, or relieve a cold's symptoms for twelve hours that great. But the purpose is incomplete until the goal is achieved – the cure is found. That purpose, the cure for the cold, will force the researchers to review, and to revise their beliefs and revalidate their values. That purpose will test their passion for staying with the task. However, until the cure is found the purpose is unfulfilled.

Sometimes a leader must recognize the greater purpose and sacrifice some victories. The leader must weigh some values higher than others, in order to achieve the greater purpose. An example of this might be the administrator who enters school administration with a strong sense of what is "right" and what is "wrong." This leader has operated under the belief system very well at this previous level of responsibility. However, at the school principal's level, this administrator encountered another concept. It was the concept of the legal settlement. The concept expanded with his duties as Superintendent of schools because lawsuits and insurance companies redefined "right" and "wrong." In many situations what was right or wrong had to be overruled by the driving question of "how much will it cost to settle this?" A student running down a staircase falls and breaks his arm. The parent blames the school because no one was supervising the hallway. All the rules are posted clearly "No running in the halls," but the student disregarded the posted rule. The parent files a lawsuit and the insurer of the school recommends paying the medical bills and cost of additional expenses. Even though the school wants to hold its ground, the insurance representatives settle out of court.

Compromising one's beliefs or changing ones values is a tough reality to accept when one enters the business to do the right thing for the students, the community and the school. When one must compromise his previously accepted beliefs, the leader is forced to seriously revisit the purpose for being in the job. If doing the right thing for children is the overall purpose, the leader can give in to the insurance settlement knowing there are more important fights to be won for children. That greater purpose has to influence the leader's beliefs, values and passion and the leader must communicate these choices in such a way that the followers recognize the efficacy of the decision.

Courage:

Courage is the strand in the rope of leadership that is essential for withstanding tough leadership challenges. Knowledge is important for the leader and followers, but without courage the effectiveness of a leader's knowledge is limited. The leader has to have courage to demonstrate it to the followers. Margaret J. Wheatley, founder of the Berkana Institute of Leadership Development, said it best when she said, "I think the greatest source of courage is to realize that if we don't act, nothing will change for the better. Reality doesn't change itself. It needs us to act..."

The reality of Public Education was changed by the federal law which was passed in 2001 that mandates "We must leave no child behind." This is a great concept and the law has noble intentions. One of the best features of the law is the requirement to disaggregate student test data and the mandate that each subgroup of students must be successful. The sub group's mandate is good because for the first time all children are expected to achieve some level of learning. Now the question is, "do educational and political leaders have the courage to fund the requirements of the law?" Prioritizing and funding this law will be an act of courage. Educational and political leaders will have to believe that all children can learn, and value this educational goal as a high fiscal responsibility. They will have to have the passion to persevere the goal of educating children – even those who are more difficult and expensive to teach. And these leaders must have the courage to overcome the critics.

To paraphrase the teachings of the late Dr. Ron Edmunds, who lead the effective schools research at Michigan State University, "we already know everything we need to know to educate all the children whose education is of value to us. The only question is why haven't we done so already?"

Courage is a powerful strand of the leadership rope because it demands action. Courage is defined and identified in action. A soldier does not win the medal of valor by talking about war. The soldier wins it by acting heroically in battle. If a leader creates a rope without the strand of courage built into it, the rope will be a weak rope. This rope would hold up some days when the sun was shining, but it would disappear when the storm appeared. It would only work when it was safe to be outside. While this rope of leadership could do limited action, it would not be appropriate for fighting the hard battles or going to war.

When a leader assumes the rope of leadership, the leader is saying he/she believes the assignment and values the cause. The leader has passion and purpose to accomplish the objective. This leader who is willing to stand up for the victory and take action to achieve it. One of the great positive benefits of demonstrating courage is the ability to welcome change. It takes courage to break from the status quo and change the way things are done.

Senator John McCain in a work with Mark Salter, <u>Of Faith of My Fathers, Worth the Fighting For, and Why Courage Matters,</u> said that during his 2000 campaign for President he failed to say that the confederate flag that flew over the state capitol of South Carolina should be taken down. He rationalized, in a moment of cowardice, that the decision should be left to the people of South Carolina and apologized, after the fact, that he failed to demonstrate the courage to do the right thing. He learned a valuable lesson from that experience. He learned that in the long run, one is far better off taking the courageous path. McCain said he did not know if he would have won South Carolina if he would have stood against the flying of the Confederate Flag, but by not doing the right thing he lost faith with his values.

Senator McCain has strong feelings and convictions about courage. He believes that fear is a condition of courage.

He says,

> One thing we can claim with complete confidence
> is that fear is indispensable to courage, fear must
> always be present for courage to exist. You must
> be afraid to have courage, suffering is not, by
> itself, courage; choosing to suffer what we fear is.
> And yet, too great a distinction is made between
> moral courage and physical courage. They are
> in many instances the same. For either to be
> authentic, it must encounter fear and prove itself
> superior to that fear. By fear, I mean the kind
> that entails serious harm to ourselves, physical
> or otherwise, the kind that wars with our need to
> take action but which we overcome because we
> value something or someone more than our own
> well-being. Courage is not the absence of fear,
> but the capacity to act despite our fears.[2]

This position was the same as Mark Twain when he said,
"Courage is not the lack of fear. It is acting in spite of it." The
rope of leadership is stronger because of the strand of courage.
Clair Booth Luce was right when she said, "Courage is the ladder
on which all the other virtues mount."

Vision:

Vision is the last strand in the rope of leadership. Vision is
the holistic sum of the leader's beliefs, values, purpose, passion
and courage. Vision is the strand which weaves in the direction
where the leader will take his/her followers. Vision is a key part

of the rope of leadership because it provides the inspiration and direction the leader needs to focus the followers toward a goal. Vision is the strand in the leadership rope which motivates the followers to act.

However, vision alone is not enough. There has to be a plan to make the vision come true. *A vision without a plan is just an hallucination.* There are many leaders with a vision, but the successful leader has a plan and the skills and talents to follow the plan making the vision a reality.

One major problem with leadership today is lack of vision and too much focus on the bottom line. In his book On Becoming A Leader, Warren Bennis said "Too many Americans believe that the bottom line isn't everything, but the only thing, and America is strangling on that lack of vision," The bottom line in business is short-term profits and long-term survival. In education, the bottom line is standardized test scores, accountability and graduation rates. However, the real vision for education is the comprehensive preparation of students for successful performance in vocations, avocations, social interactions and our democratic way of life. Leadership is aimless without a shared vision.

A key element of the vision strand in the rope of leadership is communication. To be an effective leader in education, politics, business, sports, or any endeavor one must have good communication. The leader has to sell the vision to others. This is frequently achieved through verbal and/or visual means. The commonly used verbal presentation has to be clearly communicated in words and languages the followers understand

and can identify within their daily communications. The leader could use force, persuasion, visuals, slogans, facts, figures, and other supporting information. In some situations the leader's dominance (physically, financially, educationally or politically) is great enough to hook the initial followers. John Kennedy's persona and style caught the attention of an entire nation. Dr. King's physical presence was not in itself captivating, but once he started to talk one could see him grow taller with each word. His words caught his audience and demanded attention.

An audience can easily identify leaders who are just going through the motions. The leader sells the rope with the vision in such a way that the followers are willing to hold on and press forward. There has to be proof that the leader's actions match their words before others will follow them. If leaders fail to successfully communicate their vision very few people will follow them. The followers will not take the rope unless the leader identifies how this leadership will help them to achieve the shared vision. Followers must be motivated and inspired to hold the rope, and to believe in the rope and take ownership and responsibility for the rope.

No one means of communication will work effectively for all followers. So the leader must know the followers and their interest in the vision. The leader has to find different ways to communicate or illustrate the vision. The leader should never assume that the vision is clear to all followers. Communicating the vision is a never-ending part of the rope of leadership. The leader has to maintain the connection with the followers and the connection is the rope of leadership. The common beliefs, values, passion, purpose and courage brings the vision to life for the followers.

The importance of the vision cannot be over estimated. The leader has to believe it and inspire the followers to believe it. Great leaders are able to make the rope and the vision one. In the world of athletes, one can not think of the hard work of the team, without thinking of the vision of winning. As a matter of fact some psychologists and therapists have told athletes visualize the ball going through the net or they tell track sprinters to visualize or see themselves crossing the finish line breaking the tape as part of their preparation to win their games. This technique requires the players to have a vision of their victory. This is meant to motivate and eliminate negative thoughts or distractions. Great coaches will not allow players to disconnect the preparation from the winning. Winning could range from achieving one's personal best to victory in the competition. Played out to its ultimate conclusion winning becomes the rope climbed to the ultimate victory. Only winners can qualify to compete for the prize. In life this rope is called success.

During the Civil Rights campaign people were told to "keep your eyes on the prize." They were told that they might have to suffer today, but keep looking at the prize and eventually they would achieve the justice and equality they sought. That vision of the prize of justice and equality sustained and re-energized the followers. The rope of leadership connects the leader with the followers and to the vision or prize. The message is believe in the leader, believe in the rope, believe in each other, and believe in the vision or victory. The vision strand in the rope of leadership is the glue. It unites and motivates the leader and the followers.

CHOOSING THE BEST ROPE FOR THE JOB

Ropes come in different sizes and colors. They are made in a variety of lengths with various capacities of strength and weight bearing. The most important decision a rope buyer makes is choosing the right rope for the job. It is essential to know why the rope is needed and which rope will successfully allow the user to complete the job. For example, it does not make sense to buy an expensive rope with major strength, heat resistance and abrasion resistance simply to bind wood for storage. However, if the rope will be used for climbing the face of a mountain, the mountain climber will want a rope made of the best and strongest materials. The rope must be matched with the job for which it will be used. The success of the endeavor could depend on choosing the right rope.

This same principle is true in selecting the best rope of leadership. The strands of the rope of leadership are beliefs, values, passion, purpose, courage and vision. However, the length of the rope varies to accommodate the requirements of the job.

The Length of Leadership Ropes

There are three basic lengths of ropes of leadership. They are the Short Rope, Medium Rope and Long Rope. These lengths allow leaders to utilize the rope that is best for each unique leadership opportunity.

Short Rope of Leadership

The strands of the short rope are tightly intertwined for maximum support and service. This rope relies heavily on the strands of beliefs, purpose, values and passion to reinforce the rope. The leader uses this short rope length in situations which are new and that require close supervision and instruction. A high school principal beginning a job at a new high school, or the manager of a new team of employees or even the parents of a new baby would have to consider this short rope of leadership.

The short rope of leadership involves the responsibilities of assessment and communication. It allows the leader to survey and ascertain information from the followers about the strength of the organization, and opportunities for improvement. It allows the leader to look around and listen. Finally, it allows the leader to create a plan of action and a vision for the organization.

The short rope of leadership is tightly tied to leader involvement. The leader facilitates meetings and coordinates activities because the leader knows there is only one "first chance" to make an impression. This short rope allows the leader to share beliefs, expectations and the vision early and clearly with the followers. With the short rope the leader will be able to set the tone and expectation for the operations and be visible and available for the followers. The short rope gives the leader the opportunity to demonstrate skills in communication, organization and collaboration while creating an open, invitation climate. The leader with the short rope makes every staff meeting a professional development opportunity. With the short rope of leadership, the leader can get out and meet parents, patrons and influential persons in the community. The leader will be able to respond to any concerns quickly and as appropriately as possible.

The Short-Rope-of-Leadership allows the leader to operate in a mode of high consideration and high structure. Followers are held closer to the leader because the vision is not fully defined and not yet ready to be fully shared. The vision is developing, but the leader demonstrates strong beliefs, values, passion, purpose and courage. There is little doubt among the followers that the leader has a plan to improve the organization. The Short-Rope-of-Leadership style results in more "check-with-me" mandates than longer leadership ropes, as well as more meetings, more questions, more communications about beliefs, values and expectations; more observations; more assessments; and more feedback.

However, this short rope is strong and the leader ties knots in the rope to give the followers added grip. These knots represent signs of safety and caring. The knot of safety is a net to catch the followers whose hands grow wet from the stress of added responsibilities because of the leader's high expectations. This net includes reassurances, one-on-one meetings, in-service options, mentoring, coaching, job counseling and resource options. The knot of caring allows the followers to see that the leader cares enough to provide extra support and consideration.

This knot is the first step in building trust between the leader and the follower.

Medium Rope of Leadership

The strands of the Medium Rope of Leadership are tight, but the rope is longer. There are extra strands of courage and purpose to strengthen the rope. The leader has effectively communicated the vision and the followers are holding the rope. There have been no serious tests of the follower's faith and trust in the rope, but through teaching, sharing, communications and normal operations, the followers have demonstrated positive support for the leader.

An example of a leader using the medium rope of leadership would be that of a Superintendent of a school corporation in his/her third year of service to the school district. This Superintendent has already created a strategic plan and it is in the second year of implementation. The teachers and staff support of the leader's beliefs, values, purpose and vision for the district. The community has developed a growing trust in the Superintendent's ability to lead. The Superintendent believes most employees and parents have picked up the rope.

Activities for this Superintendent would include active District Advisory meetings with fewer meetings with staff and community members that would be necessary with a shorter rope of leadership. This Superintendent will assign staff to handle most district meetings. There will be an emphasis on frequent visits to schools and district activities.

There will be annual meetings and progress reports on the district strategic plan and fewer education materials and study sessions with school board members than was necessary with the shorter rope of leadership.

A pattern of communication to parents and community members about district activities and achievements will have emerged. There will be more meetings and communications with the local Chamber of Commerce, service clubs, legislators and influential community leaders.

The Medium Rope of Leadership model provides the followers with less structure, but high consideration and attention. The rope is longer than the short rope and it allows followers to be a greater distance from the leader, but the common vision of the rope still binds them. The medium rope allows the leader more freedom with the followers and time to refine and improve the vision. The medium rope allows opportunities to incorporate change into the vision and involve more followers to be assigned to the leader because now there is more rope to hold onto. With the medium rope there will be fewer assessments, but more specific assessment indicators. There will be time to build in emergency practices for crisis situations. Finally, there will be time to develop greater trust among the followers and between the followers and the leader.

The Medium Rope of Leadership should eliminate quick decisions and diffuse crisis situations with less stress and more effectiveness. It should allow the leader to build the organization, increase ownership of the vision and develop new leaders in the organization. This type of leadership does not assume that the followers all know the vision, but it operates under the assumption that if the followers do not know the vision, they will have to learn it to stay in the organization.

The Long Rope of Leadership

The Long Rope of Leadership operates upon the knowledge that the entire organization has total ownership of the vision. The rope of leadership and the vision of victory are completely accepted by the leader and the followers. The leader leads with low structure because the followers know and understand their roles and low consideration because the followers own the rope and the vision as much as the leader. Very few leaders have the opportunity to utilize the long rope kind of leadership.

Some features of the Long Rope of Leadership are fewer meetings involving the leader than with the previous leadership ropes. This is because the followers have been educated and trained to assume their specific roles. Too many meetings would compromise the trust that has been built. There are no loner strategic plans of three to five years. Now there are teaching communities to deal with problems in short spans of time.

The vision and the rope is the same and both are subject to change. Leadership is consistently dynamic. The leader now leads leaders. New followers are rapidly empowered to assume responsibility and ownership in the rope and the vision.

The rope is long, but the communication is effectively conducted. Problems are shared with teams of leaders and the leader has complete trust in their ability. All meetings are professional development opportunities. "I will learn" is the only acceptable response.

The strands in The Long Rope of Leadership are wide and strong. They do not need closeness for strength because strength is found in the followers' and leaders' trust in the rope and the vision. This might seem like something from the future, but it is not. There are many leaders exercising the Long Rope of Leadership style today.

Dr. William G. Ouchi describes this theory in his book, <u>Making Schools Work</u>, Ouchi suggests that schools that perform best have the most decentralized management systems – individual principals control school budgets and personnel. The principals are fully responsible and fully accountable for the performance of their school. They have greater freedom and flexibility to shape their educational programs, hire specialists as needed and generally determine the direction of the school.

Summary:

The rope of leadership is defined through the beliefs, values, passion, courage, purpose and vision of the leader. The leader has to effectively and successfully communicate these strands of the rope to the followers. The rope forged by the leader and held onto the followers is the essential means to achieve the vision or victory. Therefore, the leader has to motivate and inspire the followers to take ownership of the rope.

Leaders utilize different ropes to successfully work

with followers. The short rope allows high structure, attention and consideration. It is used to work effectively in a new job or position. It enables the leader to demonstrate skills in communication, coordination, supervision, evaluation and team building. The medium rope provides high consideration and attention, but less structure or supervision. This leadership allows the leader to give up many supervisory roles and spend more time on developing ownership and creating new leaders. The Long Rope enables the leader to provide little structure or supervision and less attention and consideration because the followers are now owners of the rope and leaders in pursuing the vision. It is essential for the leader to use the right rope of leadership. This makes it fundamental for the leader to know the followers and their needs.

The rope is the key connection between the leader and the followers. It has to be strong and appropriate for the job. The leader's task is to forge the rope, choose the right length and share ownership of the rope with the followers.

References:

1. King, M. L., Jr. (1963). <u>Strength to love</u>. Cleveland, Ohio: Collins and World.
2. McCain, J. & Salter, M. (2003). <u>Of faith of my fathers, worth the fighting for, and why courage matters</u>.

CHAPTER THREE

EXCUSE #1: PEOPLE

"My Followers Fail To Hold Onto My Rope of Leadership"

"They Must Be Made To Realize That If They Succeed, The Team Succeeds, And If The Team Succeeds, They Succeed."

Vince Lombardi

THE FOLLOWERS

"Pick Up the Rope and Follow Me"

One of the most common excuses given by unsuccessful leaders is that the followers are the problem. These "would-be" leaders indicate that if they just had the "right" people or "their" people, the job would get done.

Relationships

There is no such thing as leadership without followers. Followers define leadership. In reality, followers will make or break a leader. There are five universal principles that I have learned about leading people:

1. Followers want to know their leader cares about them.

   People want to feel valued and appreciated. This is why the leader's rope or vision for the leadership task is so important. People need something in which to believe and in which to participate. They generate a sense of self worth or importance from what they do. There is a great difference in just carrying bricks everyday on the job site as opposed to carrying bricks to build a cathedral. This is especially true if the brick carrier is Catholic. The leader defines why carrying the bricks is vital to the success of the project. The leader can make that brick carrier feel as important as the brick mason if the rope is right. The person carrying the bricks needs something to hold on to. He needs something to add value to his participation.

The amazing thing is that many people really do not know how much they need to feel appreciated. A good leader will tell them, but a great leader will show them. Leaders must get followers involved in the planning, organizing and collaboration of the job or goal. Research reminds us about the physiological and safety needs of workers. Satisfying only these needs is not enough. Leaders must find ways to make followers feel valued and needed. Leaders must provide them with opportunities to increase their involvement and ownership in the whole process. Leaders must believe that people can be creative, self-directed and motivated. Leaders must eliminate fear. Fear is distracting and it prevents people from thinking productively.

2. Followers are not ultimately motivated by money.

Money will not buy loyalty or ownership. The leader has to provide something greater than money to generate ownership, loyalty and passion for the task at hand. William F. Whyte, in his research on industrial relations, found that money is not as strong a motivational tool as many were led to believe.[1] This was especially true for production workers. For many of the workers in Whyte's study, their peer group was the greatest motivator. Whyte estimated that only about 10 percent of the production workers in the United States would ignore group pressure and produce as much as possible in response to an incentive plan. Whyte found that workers were more concerned about the opinions of their fellow workers, their personal comfort and enjoyment on the job, and their long-range security than just extra money from an incentive plan.

Saul W. Gellerman said that the most subtle and most important characteristic of money is its power as a symbol. This is characterized by its market value. It is what money can buy, not money itself that gives it value. However, money has additional meaning beyond market value. Money can symbolize almost anything people want it to mean. Money motivates people at the basic or lower levels of need. These needs pertain to safety, security, food, and shelter. However, when the lower basic needs and material needs have been satisfied or satiated, money loses its ability to motivate higher performance.

In the National Basketball Association (NBA) where most players are millionaires and their basic needs are satisfied, one often hears them say they are motivated to improve their game because they want to "Be Like Mike" or even better. The Holy Grail of motivation is the NBA Championship ring. Gary Payton and Carl Malone gave up millions of dollars to join the Los Angeles Lakers in pursuit of "the ring." During the 2003-2004 NBA season Carl Malone a future "Hall of Famer" and longtime Utah Jazz player chose to play with the Los Angeles Lakers for the minimum salary of one million dollars in hopes of finally winning a championship. Gary Payton, another future "Hall of Famer" opted to leave his team of many years, the Seattle Supersonics, and take minimum salary to seek a championship with the Los Angeles Lakers. Money wasn't the motivator for either of them, but the championship was. Unfortunately even with them the Lakers lost to Detroit. Money is very important, but it is not the final answer for truly motivating people.

Sometimes followers and leaders share a common goal or purpose. This goal or purpose could range from fighting for the right to vote to civil rights. These common goals or purposes serve to motivate followers to hold the rope and follow the leader. It is often said that the United States has more unity and is closer to its ideals during times of conflict or crisis. These kinds of events motivate people to work together for a common purpose. This kind of motivation goes beyond what money can buy.

3. <u>Followers appreciate leaders who practice what they preach.</u>

Setting the example is better than telling the example. Action does speak louder than words. Mahatma Gandhi said, "You must be the change you wish to see in the world." When we increase responsibility and provide challenging work with the appropriate support and consideration, people tend to do great things. A leader has to model the appropriate risk-taking example needed in the organization. When something is wrong good leaders address the issue. In seeking solutions the leader should involve followers in the process as often as possible. Followers have a vested interest in the success of the leader and involving followers increases their ownership in the rope or vision. The leader should exercise care and caution when dealing with people's problems. When followers fail to meet expectations, it's wise and considerate to show disappointment, but demonstrate a desire to help them correct the problem. Involve them in developing strategies or ways to correct the situation.

4. <u>Follower's performance will rise to the level of the leader's expectations.</u>

Leaders will get the performance they expect to get. If leaders expect less, they will often receive less. I have come to believe that it is better to commence relationships with followers by communicating my expectations of them and what they can expect from me. This is followed by clearly communicating the ground rules, consequences and options. This is a "close" supervision or short rope approach, but it is modified to fit various situations as our relationship develops through shared experiences, assignments, tasks and assessments. I think it is unwise to assign significant responsibility to followers without understanding that many of these followers expect me to tell them what to do. However, once they have been orientated, educated and had some experience in the assigned area, I expect them to be ready to take the lead.

Followers cannot perform their jobs unless they know what to do. Supervisors cannot supervise what they do not know. Children cannot learn what the teachers do not teach. Employees cannot grow if employers do not know how to evaluate and supervise them. There can really be no expectations for excellence until people know what they are expected to accomplish. To expect the best from employees and their supervisors means that there can be no assumptions. A leader must assess, provide professional development, evaluate and elevate. My expectations of employees are based upon the belief that if they know better, they will do better and my job is to ensure that they know better. Leaders have to ensure that employees never stop learning. There are too many challenges to meet to be unprepared.

5. Followers must respect the leadership of the leader

If a leader wants to be loved, he should buy a dog! To be successful, leaders must develop positive relationships with their followers. However, positive relationships are not necessarily friendships. The leader will have to make some difficult decisions and many of these decisions will involve the followers. The leader cannot get too close to followers because it might compromise the leader's ability to make an appropriate decision when the time comes. As a school superintendent, I base all decisions on what is best for the children. I allow this goal to serve as the compass or foundation of all that is done in the school district. Doing what is best for the children is the bond that holds the fibers of my leadership rope. This goal focuses my actions with administrators, teachers, parents, students and community patrons. Considering what is best for the children also guides my involvement with contractors and vendors.

Such decisions as issues of redistricting, teacher dismissal, termination of an administrator, legal threats, lawsuits, parental threats, politics, negotiations, or disagreements with school board members can make leadership at the superintendent's level a lonely place. However, if a leader remembers that the primary goal is not to be loved, but to serve fairly and conscientiously, one can grow from these unique opportunities. I am always reminded of the old saying that "everything that's popular is not right, and everything that's right is not popular."

Followers Are the Key

Jim Collins' research, in his book Good To Great, puts the old adage "people are your most important asset" to rest. The "right people" are the leader's most important asset. Collins recommends that the first thing that leaders must do is to get the right people on the bus. Therefore, leaders must actively work to improve the performance of the people already on the bus. It can be done and it must be done if the leader hopes to be successful and effective. Followers or people are essential to a leader, and they define the personal power of a leader. The leader is wise to identify the style of the people he/she wants as followers. The success and effectiveness of the relationship and production of the leader and the followers will depend on how well the leader adapts his/her style to the followers or how well the followers' styles can be adapted to fit the leader's style. There has to be some adjustment on the part of the leader and/or followers. Victor H. Vroom, in his work   Some Personality Determinants of the Effects of Participation, uncovered evidence to suggest that the effectiveness of a leader is dependent largely on the style of the individual workers. He said,

> Place a group with strong independence drives under a supervisor who needs to keep his men under his thumb and the result is very likely to be trouble. Similarly, if you take docile men who are accustomed to obedience and respect for their supervisors and place them under a supervisor who tries to make them manage their own work, they are likely to wonder uneasily whether he really knows what he is doing.[2]

The following example shows how the rope of leadership metaphor illustrates Vroom's point. There is a group of followers who know what is expected of them, and have taken ownership of their leadership rope. They understand the expectations of their leader. They do not need the leader watching them constantly or checking to make sure that they are holding the rope properly. They are medium rope followers. Place these followers with a new leader who has no trust in their ability to hold the rope and is constantly checking on them. He is a short rope leader. Soon there will be a problem because the followers who had been allowed to carry a medium length rope and operate with trust and ownership are now on a short rope, and the leader is closely watching them all the time.

Conversely, there is a group of followers who have been operating under a leader with a short rope with constant checks and assessments. Then these followers are placed with a leader who has a long rope style, who allows them greater freedom with less attention and supervision. When this long rope leader tries to give them ownership of the rope, problems occur because these followers think that the leader does not care as much about them, or they think that the new leader may not know how to do the job. Leadership styles and the styles of followers must be adjusted or altered to fit the situation.

The leader's rope has to be strong enough to connect the followers to the leader's style or expectations. It has to override or exceed the fears and concerns of the followers. Conversely the leader has to utilize practices that are compatible with the needs of the followers. Leaders should not expect followers to change overnight. Before change can occur, there must be orientation and education, plus time for practice. However, these situations vary from leader to leader. When Bill Parcells took control of the Dallas Cowboys Football team in 2003, there was a short turn-around time for change. Parcells used the short rope style: appropriate steps of orientation with expectations, modeling, and clear rules and consequences. As a result, he took a team from the bottom of the Eastern Conference to the play-offs in one year. There would be a problem with this type of leadership however, if the rope always remains short.

I have seen school principals do the same thing as Bill Parcells. In each situation, these principals respected their followers enough to clearly get to know their styles and practices. Then these leaders initiated their expectations. In each case, these leaders communicated the idea that failure was not an option. They expected progress and the followers knew what the leader had to do to improve the situation. Followers respect and respond to leaders who clearly communicate expectations, responsibilities, rules and consequences.

Blaming leadership failure on poor followers is a legitimate reason why leadership fails. There is no leadership without people. Some people are better to work with than others, but leaders have to work with all kinds of people.

MOTIVATION

The primary factor in getting followers to follow the leader is motivation. There are numerous kinds of motivation. Motivation causes followers to have an attitude of cooperation. Motivation is directly connected to the followers' needs. These needs could be tangible such as personal gain, compensation, safety, rewards, security, or money. Other followers will be motivated by such intangible feelings as revenge, love, hate, beliefs, spiritual callings, political dynamics, or a desire to achieve ideals like saving or spreading democracy, or protecting one's country. Personal interest creates motivation to follow the leader who will enable the followers to achieve personal success. The rope of the leader has to connect with the needs of the followers.

There are some leaders with ropes or visions so powerful that the followers' needs become secondary to the needs of the leader. The leader's rope can sometimes be strong enough to elevate the followers beyond their needs to a higher level of commitment. These leaders are commonly called inspirational leaders because they touch a deeper core of consciousness within the followers. Former UCLA Hall of Fame Basketball Coach John Wooden had high school All-American basketball players coming to UCLA to play and win national championships. These talented young men were motivated to be a part of a big time winning program, but what they did not know was that to become a champion on this grand stage, they would have to change. They could not all shoot the ball at the same time and they could not all play at the same time. Someone had to sit on the bench and support the five players on the floor. John Wooden inspired them to put the team ahead of their personal interests and goals. They became followers of a philosophy larger than themselves. He inspired them with his record of successful victories and championships; he inspired them with his personal discipline and the expectations and rules generated from his discipline; he inspired them with his knowledge and how he taught them to play the game; and he inspired them with his vision and plan for success. He called it his "pyramid of success."[3]

Motivating followers is not always easy. If people have no goals, no desires, no dreams, no aspirations or needs, it is very difficult for any leader to motivate them to follow. Leaders must be able to connect the followers to the rope and the success and possibilities gained from holding the rope. In other words, the leaders must inform followers of what they will gain from holding onto the leader's rope and how their needs, wants, and dreams will be achieved. If followers are not motivated to follow the leader there has to be a face-to-face meeting to ascertain why. If there is no positive agreement or plan created at the meeting, the leader has to find a way to allow the person to leave the organization.

General Dwight D. Eisenhower, who later became the President of the United States, demonstrated the art of leadership with a simple piece of string. He would put the string on a table and say, "pull it and it'll follow wherever you wish. Push it and it will go nowhere at all." It is just that way in leading people. Pushing and prodding people rarely gets the best out of them. People who work for prodders have little incentive to do more than just get by. All they want to do is to keep the leader "off their backs." Effective leaders get more out of people by working with them and helping them to do their best. Positive associations with followers are very valuable. A leader cannot develop these associations without getting involved with the followers. Leaders cannot sit in the stands and watch the action because leadership is a contact sport. Leadership is about leading people and leading people is about relationships.

Leaders can create a motivating climate and inspire followers by utilizing the following practices. Leaders should:

1. *Set high expectations and model the behavior they expect from their followers.* Leaders are always on stage and followers want to see what the leaders do and how they respond in crisis and unexpected emergency situations.

2. *Give clear instructions and expectations for all assignments.* Make sure the followers know what is expected of them in general and in dealing with specific assignments or tasks.

3. *Provide meaningful work and assignments for followers and eliminate as much "grunt" work as possible.* Keep followers interest high by providing as much variety and responsibility as possible.

4. *When possible, listen to the views and opinions of followers.* Respect and support "thinking" by followers. Learn to listen and not to automatically give a response. In others words, instead of thinking of what to say next to a follower, stop, listen and think about what the follower is really saying.

5. *Give praise and feedback to followers for their work.* When followers fall short of expectations, reassure them that the goal is still achievable and urge them to

try again. Be sure to tell them why they failed to get the job done and suggest ways for them to get it done properly the next time. Leaders must understand the value of demonstrating appreciation appropriately for followers.

6. *Expand the decision making process to include more followers whenever possible.* Expanded decision making increases ownership. Seek the advice and opinions of followers and give credit to others as often as possible.

7. *Respect followers because they are essential to your leadership efforts.* Find the dignity and value in the work of followers and celebrate their efforts.

HOLDING THE ROPE

While most followers are motivated to hold onto the rope of leadership because their needs are being met, there are some followers who hold onto the rope because they love the cause which is represented by the rope. In other words, some followers follow leaders because their beliefs and values match the message, vision or rope of the leader. There are followers of Nelson Mandela who have never been to South Africa. They have never endured the pain, misery and deprivation of apartheid. However, they love freedom, justice, liberation and liberty. They admire bravery and courage in the face of impossible circumstances. They believe in what Mandela believed and they hold the rope of Mandela's vision. Sometimes followers connect with leaders because they share a common cause or philosophy and the inspiration is greater than motivation for personal gain.

These two rationales of self interest and love of the vision or rope, are why followers follow leaders. I have found few followers who follow for no apparent reason. Followers are seekers and they expect the leader to fulfill their desires, needs, and aspirations.

WHY FOLLOWERS DROP THE ROPE

The easy answer to the question, "Why do followers drop the rope?" is simple. The followers lose their reason to hold on. Followers will not continue to hold the rope and believe in the leader if they forget why they took the rope in the first place. Leaders have to continue to maintain a relationship with followers and continue to stress the importance of holding the rope. The best way to examine why followers drop the rope is to look closely at the key connections that bond the leader and the followers to the rope. There are four basic dis-connectors:

1. Followers lose trust in their leader.
   One of the most important connections between the leader and the follower is trust. The initial bond of the rope of leadership between the leader and the followers is the

development of confidence and reliance. The followers believe, accept and rely on the message, words, and actions of the leader. The followers open themselves to the possibilities and opportunities generated from the leader. They believe and develop trust in the leader. They accept and tightly hold the rope of the leader. When trust is compromised, the relationship between the leader/the rope/ and the followers changes. When trust is destroyed there is no rope to be held and no reason to seek the rope. The American Public dropped President Richard Nixon's leadership rope after the "Watergate Scandal." Public validated evidence clearly illustrated that the President had lied repeatedly to the American public. The leader-followers relationship was broken because we could no longer trust the President.

2. <u>Followers do not feel supported by their leader.</u>

Followers whose leaders are apt to back away or bail out when faced with problems, leaving followers in the lurch or turn to blaming them and criticizing their actions are hard pressed to continue to follow their leader. Lacking the support needed to get the job done, they become extremely cautious in taking on new tasks or jobs that may involve problems. They seek the safest course of action. Instead of playing to win, they play not to lose. This compromises their effectiveness. Backing followers does not mean playing games to please them or telling them they are right when they are wrong. However, it does mean sharing part of the responsibility for defeats, sharing the blame for poor performance and helping followers to do a better job. It means being there to support them through the good times as well as the bad. When followers do not feel valued and supported, they will not value or support their leader. This causes a breakdown in the relationship. Followers support leaders who support them.

3. <u>Followers see their leaders lack courage.</u>
   Rudy Giuliani said "A leader must be willing to do things and say things that people may not like. Telling difficult truths is an important part of helping people manage their fears or threats from layoffs to violence." Followers want their leader to do the right thing. They believe and trust in the integrity of their leader and they want that loyalty to be demonstrated by the actions of the leader. It is essential

for followers to know that the leader has their best interest in mind. This kind of trust builds a strong bond and ownership in the rope of leadership. When leaders fail to demonstrate courage, followers question the leadership. Leaders demand respect by being up front and communicating truthfully with the followers. When followers hear different stories from the leader and find the leader playing games, the relationship is compromised and the rope of leadership is weakened. A lack of courage by the leader is a motivator for dropping the rope. Followers respect a leader who tackles the tough problems and makes the tough decisions.

4. <u>Followers are given too many ropes.</u>

The vision, mission or rope can be revised or adjusted, but it seldom can be replaced without compromising the relationship between the leader/the rope/and the followers. When leaders are unsure of their direction and make frequent changes and revisions to the rope or even replace the rope with a different vision, problems develop for followers. Change is too important to occur haphazardly. Mahatma Gandhi could not advocate non-violence one month and physical aggression the next month without losing many followers. Too many ropes to hold results in no rope to hold. Change always compromises the interest of some followers. Followers want a leader with clear vision of where to go and how to get there.

GIVING FOLLOWERS SOMETHING TO HOLD ON TO

Leaders can never take their followers for granted. The rope could be strong and the relationship between the leader and followers could be solid, but there are no guarantees or unbreakable connections. Production totals, legal requirements, company procedures and guidelines all change. Companies change ownership, jobs are consolidated and staffs are reduced. These changes can all contribute to the strength of the leadership rope. Leaders must understand that followers need to be nurtured through these changes. Clear and timely communication is essential for reducing fear and false rumors. Whether the news is good or bad, the followers want to hear it from the leader. In a fall edition of Sports Illustrated, Warren Sapp makes this point when he describes how he felt about being traded from the Tampa Bay Buccaneers to the Oakland Raiders. Sapp says he was very disappointed with the lack of communication by his former Coach John Gruden. He said, "There's no animosity. The only thing that sets me on edge is that for all the time me and

Gruden spent face-to-face, he didn't have the nuts to say, Warren you just ain't in our plans anymore. I would've took that a lot better than no call at all." Followers want a leader who accepts responsibility and shares the blame for the outcome.

The leader's vision or rope connects the followers to the leader. Together the leader, followers and the rope form a tremendous synergy for change and success. The rope creates an essential conduit of reciprocity between the leader and the followers.

Summary

Leaders sometimes see followers as the excuse for failing to achieve successful leadership, but there is no leadership without people. People define leadership. Leaders have to develop positive relationships with followers and sell them the vision or plan of their leadership rope. People want leaders to care about them. Money is important to followers but it will not buy loyalty or ownership in the leader's vision or rope. Followers want leaders to set the example by their actions even more than their words. Leaders get what they expect to get from followers. Leaders should never assume that followers know what to do. Leaders have to ensure that followers know the vision, plan, expectations, assessments and most of all, what value the follower will receive from holding a particular leader's rope. Knowing what value they will receive is motivational for followers. People are motivated to follow leaders for self interest and/or love of the vision or rope. People seldom blindly follow the leader. They have defined reasons or needs to follow.

Followers drop the leader's rope when they lose trust in the leader or vision; when leaders fail to support them; when the leader lacks the courage to do the right things; and when the leader has too many ropes to hold. Leaders get followers to hold the rope when they: do not take them for granted and communicate with them in a clear and timely manner; when the leader and followers share a common goal; when the leader and followers work to solve problems together; and when the leader gets followers to know that he is with them and has their best interest at heart. The right followers are the most important asset for a successful and effective leader.

References:

1. Whyte, W. F. (1955). <u>Money and motivation</u>. New York: Harper & Row, Publishers.

2. Vroom, V. H. (1960). <u>Some personality determinants of the effects of participation</u>. Englewood, Cliffs, New Jersey: Prentice Hall, Inc.

3. Chapin, D. & Prugh, J. (1973). <u>The wizard of westwood</u>. New York, NY: Warner Books, Inc.

4. Collins, J. (2001). <u>Good to great</u>. New York: Harper Collins.

CHAPTER FOUR

EXCUSE #2: VISION/PLAN

"My Followers Do Not Share My Vision And Plan"

"The very essence of leadership is you have to have a vision…
You can't blow an uncertain trumpet."

Father Theodore Hesburgh,
Former President of Notre Dame University

The Plan

Another common problem in many leadership situations is a lack of vision. In reality, a lack of vision is the genesis of having no plan or a poor plan. If leaders do not know where they are going, no road will get them there.   The leader has to have a plan. The leader's rope includes the vision and the plan. It is very important to understand that a ***leader's vision without a plan is simply a hallucination.*** Many people have vision, but few of them have the plan to make the vision become a reality. For the purposes of this discussion, we will consider the vision and plan together as the focus of the leader's rope.

A new leader took over the job of plant manager in a Midwestern city and quickly discovered that things moved along with little focus or direction. Employees operated primarily by doing their isolated jobs. There was no sense of team, unity, focus, goal, or accountability in this plant. The employees had worked for four different plant managers in the last six years and they did not think the manager made any significant difference in the operation of the plant.   The results of this leadership were unsuccessful, but moderately effective.   The followers saw themselves as productive because no one had told them otherwise.   There were no production goals, no collaboration and no motivation to change.

The new manager had a vision of what the plant could be and he had a plan to achieve the vision, but he had so far been unable to implement the plan because he had not communicated the plan to the employees. This is the critical vision leadership point: If the manager owns the vision and plan, but is unable to share ownership with other employees, the rope will be dropped. The rope of leadership will not achieve success if it is only in the hands of the leader. The leader has to find ways to get the employees or followers to share the rope. These are the recommended steps to help the leader share the rope:

1. ***Find a way to share the vision/plan.*** A common practice is to meet with the followers and communicate the vision and plan. However, the key motivator in this kind of meeting is simple. The leader must sell the followers on how it will benefit them.

2. ***Get input from the followers.*** The new leader could survey the employees and ask them key questions to ascertain input. The leader should ask questions such as: What is the greatest strength of this plant? If you had the power, what would you do to improve this plant? What is in need of immediate improvement? What is the ideal production quantity for the plant? The leader can take information obtained from this kind of survey and incorporate it into the vision and plan. The leader could also organize small groups from the various areas of operations (production, shipping, public relations, union leaders, etc.) to make suggestions. Gathering input from the followers gives them a sense of ownership.

3. ***Set expectations, rules and guidelines*** and make

sure that all employees have the information.

4. **Set short term performance goals** while providing close supervision, support, solid communication and accountability.

5. **Post all results** for employees to see and study.

6. **Create quality assurance teams** for input into the production, supervision and evaluation of the product.

7. **Create ways for followers to assume more leadership** in the production, supervision and evaluation of the product.

8. **Create quality review meetings** to allow different employees to work with the leader in making the plan operations more productive.

9. **Find ways to celebrate**, recognize and compensate employees who earn the awards.

10. **Allow employees to evaluate** the leader's effectiveness for the year with recommendations for improvements.

These steps will allow the leader to share the rope with employees and develop leaders among them. Now the employees have the short rope, but when these steps have been accomplished, the followers will be ready for the leader's longer rope. The followers will be ready to take ownership in the new vision because they own the current operation.

This plant manager will improve the productivity of the plant and the employee followers will have new attitudes about their jobs and trust in the leadership. However, if the plant manager leaves before a critical number of followers have ownership in the rope and vision the new progress will be compromised because ownership takes time to build.

Vision and Environment

As I am writing this chapter, I am flying from Phoenix, Arizona to Indianapolis, Indiana. From my window seat in the emergency row of a B-737 airplane, I am observing the landscape from state to state. From this distance things are not truly what they seem at first glance. Many things are lost in the coloration of the landscape. You have to look very hard to make out objects below when you are flying at 30,000 feet.

Leaders develop vision by looking, living and learning. You must be educated to recognize what you are seeing. If you don't know about it you will have a tough time seeing it. In order to develop a vision a leader has to acquire knowledge and understanding. Once having this understanding the leader can then develop plans to make that vision come to life.

If a passenger is flying over a city that is very familiar to her, she can look out the window from great heights and recognize the land, places and objects below. Knowledge of the environment increases the ability to really see what is happening there. The twists and turns of the highway; the bend or break of the river are common happenings when you are knowledgeable about the environment. Leaders must be knowledgeable about the environment in order to improve their vision.

These observations remind me of the topography of the leadership journey that leaders must take as they work with their followers and the rope these leaders use in their journey to reach a successful goal or vision. However, during the leadership journey, leaders do not have the luxury of flying above the landscape of their circumstances. They will have to make the journey up close and personal interacting with the landscape of the leadership environment. The leader's vision and plan has to be strong enough to carry followers over the rough roads and difficult times. One of the keys to leadership is to be able to recognize where one is and how to make the appropriate adjustments when necessary.

The leader's rope (vision/plan) must be strong enough to support the followers in all landscape situations and conditions. When followers stumble and fall, the leader must offer the rope to help them back on their feet. When the land is flat and easy to travel, the leader can enjoy an unchallenged period; however, this is the perfect time to prepare for the tough times. President John F. Kennedy once said, "Prepare for war in the time of peace." It is extremely difficult to prepare for war during the battle. The leader knows that war, conflicts, and disasters will come.

No matter how flat the landscape may be in Kansas or Indiana, it will change in Colorado and Utah. Leaders must prepare the followers for the valleys, hills and mountains. It is the leader's responsibility and duty to use the rope (vision/plan) to prepare the followers for the journey, the battle, or the project. The leader's rope is the basic connection with the followers.

Followers must believe in the rope of the leader and hold tightly to it in all situations. The landscape will change and with change will come conflict, anxiety, fear and doubt. Some followers will fear the heights of the landscape. Others will fear lakes or oceans. Still others will fear the forest or desert. However, if they believe in the rope of the leader and hold on to it, they will overcome the fears created by changes in the landscape of the journey. The rope will provide a place to steady the insecure followers. If there is no vision (rope), it is very easy for followers to get lost in the landscape. If there is no vision, there is nothing for the followers to hold onto for support and direction.

Our experience in the United States with wars has taught us that our citizens will support their President and troops in campaigns against enemies who clearly are a threat to our democratic way of life, but when the danger is not clearly defined and the actions are not closely related to our interests, support waivers and gradually diminishes. World War I and World War II are vivid examples of wars that created a strong rope of connection with the U.S. citizens. There had to be sacrifices made to support the wars and both wars were necessary to protect our way of life, to protect democracy and freedom. However, the Viet Nam War never made that connection. It was never really seen as a war against our freedoms and liberties. It was in a place of unknown origin to most in the U.S. Many followers questioned why we were involved in such a war. The cost of the war grew and the death totals went higher and higher and then the anti-war backlash started to change America's view about the war. In the landscape of this war campaign, the rope was severed and U.S. citizens lost their way. The leader, President Lyndon B. Johnson, could not create a rope strong enough to hold the country together.

The more challenging the goal, the more powerful the rope needs to be. Weak ropes cannot survive the rugged terrain of war. President Johnson's rope was too weak for the mission of Viet Nam and he took a journey and made a decision for which he failed to prepare his followers. They were unprepared and lost their way. There was no vision or rope to hold.

The leader has to create the vision/plan for the organization. The core of the leader's rope is the vision and plan. It is fundamental for leaders to know that the followers have to be involved and engaged in making the vision/plan what it will ultimately become. However, before others are invited to be involved in the process of developing the vision/plan, the leader must already know what it has to be. As Stephen Covey said, the leader has to "start with the end in mind." The plant manager in the previous example knew what the plant had to become. The vision/plan was clear, but to share ownership, the leader had to develop a process which involved others in the evolution of this vision/plan. The process of involvement, inclusion, and engagement created ownership and effectively placed the leadership rope in the hands of the plant employees.

It is very important for leaders to know and understand that many persons, committees, task forces and others can develop a shared vision/plan, but the true owner is the leader. The leader can share ownership, but he/she cannot share the ultimate accountability for the vision and plan. If it succeeds, everyone is happy and owns it, but if it fails, everyone looks to the leader to own it. It is this kind of accountability that requires and demands that the leader knows and understands the vision and plan completely. Getting the company or organization from the development of the vision/plan to implementation of the vision and plan is the leader's job.

The Rope Metaphor:

The excuse of poor vision or plan is not often offered by leaders who fail to get the job done. However, their followers frequently volunteer that the lack of a plan or vision caused the leadership failure to occur.

The vision/plan is the rope of the leader. The leader has to fully understand the rope in order to share it with the followers. There is no way to convince followers to hold a rope that is not real to them. The plant manager allowed employees to help create a rope they could all hold and believe in. He extended the rope which they eventually caught hold of by showing the benefits of the rope to them. He motivated them by sharing ownership of the rope.

The leader can not get others to follow without getting them to believe in the rope or vision/plan. Every political party extends a rope for party leaders to hold and believe in. This rope becomes the parties' or candidate's platform or plank. By holding the rope and following the party leaders, the followers believe good things will happen for them. If the people refuse to hold the rope of a political party, it will die. People make the party and the rope hold the people. People want something to trust and believe in.

Summary

Leaders must have a vision and plan for the success of the organization. A lack of vision is the genesis of no plan or a poor plan. A vision without a plan is simply an hallucination. The vision and plan has to be one and together they create the focus of the leadership rope. A leader has to find ways and processes to involve others in creating a vision/plan. However, before others are involved, the leader has to have an idea and understanding of what the vision and plan must be. Input from the followers is essential because the leader needs others to share ownership of the vision/plan. The leader shares the rope with the followers and creates ways to build the relationships. In the early stages of leadership with the new rope, the leader utilizes a short rope and sets expectations, rules, guidelines, and communicates clearly and timely. Short-term performance goals with close supervision are the norm.

However, as followers catch hold of the rope and assume greater responsibility, the rope can be longer with less supervision. The leader seeks greater ownership in the rope, but he can never forget that he is accountable for the rope. The leader is accountable for the success of the vision/plan. The core strand of the rope of leadership is the vision strand. There is no rope of leadership without the vision/plan.

CHAPTER FIVE

EXCUSE #3: POLITICS

"Community and Internal Politics Interfere With My Ability to Lead."

"…Every management act is a political act."

Richard Farson

The Politics

A common response from unsuccessful leaders is to complain that the "Politics" of the community, district, company or board *just* will not allow me to do my job. Politics may appear to be unbeatable forces that prevent leadership from being successful and effective. Frequently, when one thinks of politics, one thinks of local, state and national government, but politics are much broader and more common than most people could imagine.

According to Webster's New Collegiate Dictionary, being political means "the ability to influence others in multiple ways, i.e., shrewdness in managing people, programs or activities; collaborating with others to achieve a goal or outcome; or effectively dealing with others to achieve a certain agenda, production or desired objective." Being politic or political has a great deal of application in the governmental process, but it is just as important in all facets of leadership. While I did not take a graduate course on the politics of leadership, and the politics of leadership was not a part of the formal curriculum for my degree as an Education Specialist or of my Doctoral program, I have learned from experience that politics are built into leadership. Politics means working with people and leadership is about effectively working with people. Leadership and politics go hand in hand.

Corporate chief executive officers employ experts to lobby in local, state and national legislative bodies on behalf of company interests. Chambers of commerce members actively lobby and participate in politics to enhance, protect and expand their interests. Many people understand that politics are essential to effective leadership in the corporate, private and public sectors. However, some leaders are surprised by the major role played by politics in public education at the K-12 and secondary levels. Successful leaders must become active players in the political arena. Leaders must build coalitions; work for elected or appointed boards; communicate with the public; negotiate with workers' unions and labor contracts; work with special interest groups; organize campaigns; respond to neighborhood interests or concerns; deal with environmental demands; influence local, state and national politics; seek public and private funds; pass levies; work with community power brokers; and negotiate with financial institutions. Leaders cannot be free of politics.

My colleague and friend, Steve Keith, shared an example of politics from a sermon he heard in church a few weeks ago which derived leadership principles from the Bible about dealing with local politics. The sermon was based on the pastor's discussion of Acts 16:1-21. This passage described how the apostle Paul dealt with the Jewish leaders' challenge to the apostles about whether a man had to be circumcised in order to be saved. This was a political question in that day and time. The answer to this question had huge implications for whether or not to convert the gentiles or lead them to Christ. Since the Gentiles were not circumcised, it would be highly unlikely that adult males would be willing to be circumcised in order to be saved. According to this pastor's interpretation of the text, Paul gives five steps to deal with these political issues:

1. Speak with the person(s) directly (Do not rely on others for information and do not give information to others regarding an issue. Talk directly with the people involved.)

2. Seek wise counsel. (Paul went to the other apostles and the elders to discuss this issue to help make a decision.)

3. Tell the truth, the whole truth, and nothing but the truth.

4. Refer to the Word of God. (Believe and follow the vision/plan or rope.)

5. Rely on God's word. (The vision/plan or rope will hold you and keep you focused when challenged by politics.)

This example is not here to start a dissertation or major discourse. It simply demonstrates that politics also impact biblical history and that politics are as old as "man's interaction with man." Leadership and politics go hand in hand.

David H. Auston abruptly quit as president of Case Western Reserve University during tense negotiations for a new affiliation pact between his institution and University Hospitals of Cleveland. He quit in this manner because, as he wrote, of the lack of "the full and active support of a strong and well-functioning board." Some would say that board politics forced him to resign.

Three trustees sat on the boards of both the University

and the hospitals. This included the current Case Western Board's Chairman. The dual memberships were a problem that Mr. Auston felt compromised the needs of the University during the negotiations.

In Mr. Auston's letter of resignation to the five trustees, he said the proposed agreement pushed by the trustees "unnecessarily concedes far too much" to the hospitals and would "further diminish the stature and quality" of Case Western's Medical school. "The job of university president is a very demanding one, even at the best of times," he wrote. "Without the full and active support of a strong and well-functioning board, it becomes intolerable." Mr. Auston seemed to believe that there was a clear conflict of interest in the dual roles of the three trustees. This conflict would not allow them to give their full interest and focus to the needs of Case Western Reserve University. This conflict of interest was great enough to cause a great deal of frustration in Mr. Auston. However, this might not have been his reason for resignation, but it didn't encourage him to stay.

It is hard to call Mr. Auston an unsuccessful leader because he had a great start as President of Case Western Reserve University. He had a vision and plan for the University. He met with deans, administrators and local alumni donors. He took the next several months on a nine-city tour of alumni chapters across the country. He outlined his action plan at his inauguration during his first year and highlighted his goals and plans for a capital campaign. After less than two years he quit. He said there were fundamental disagreements with the Board of Trustees. Fundamental disagreements among people is a common expression for politics. However, Mr. Auston was not an unsuccessful leader. He was a good leader who experienced an unsuccessful situation. College Presidents have to successfully work with their Board of Trustees.

Mr. Auston appeared to have strong ethics and a value system that would not allow him to compromise his vision for Case Western Reserve University. He made no excuses for his expectations, but he stated that the politics of the Board of Trustees was unacceptable. Maybe other leaders could have worked this through with the Board, but every leader has to be true to his rope and vision.

In working with the politics of Boards, it is important that leaders know that Board members are holding the leader's rope. My Board and I have an agreement that there will be no surprises in the way in which they support my decisions. In return, I will avoid surprising them with information announcements, initiatives, etc. Our agreement of "No Surprises" is not written in my contract or in the Board's by-laws. It is a verbal understanding we have agreed to follow. We have to hold each other responsible for maintaining this verbal agreement.

Communication is the key to preventing surprises. Too much information is better than too little information. Leaders cannot afford to assume what board members will do. Leaders should work with boards to create board education sessions, create board by-laws with ethics codes, conduct at least one board leadership retreat annually and work to eliminate conflicts of interest.

Mr. Auston and his board were not holding the same

rope. They simply did not share the same vision/plan for the University. Board members had other agendas or interests that possibly compromised their roles or collaboration with Mr. Auston.

There are numerous leadership situations that require political savvy. Here are three common scenarios for consideration. They are the "Right, but ...Situation;" the "Godfather Situation"; and the "Don't Rock the Boat or Else Situation." A look at these three examples illustrates some of the dynamics of politics in leadership:

1. The "Right, but..." political situation is common in leadership. It involves a decision made by the leader that is "Right" based upon the leader's decision making criteria which includes such things as consulting the data available and the best consultation recommendations. This includes making the decision which is best for the organization and employees, and/or the most cost efficient and most productive. After considering all these criteria, the leader often thinks that all considerations are aligned for a positive decision. However there is still the "but" question standing between the leader and the final decision. These "but" questions could be issues raised by the union or teachers' association, issues raised from legal considerations, issues raised by the local power brokers, or issues which arise from tradition or strong past practice. As a leader, I learned some

time ago that "being right is not always enough." Often "right" is compromised by other forces too strong to ignore. Nevertheless the character and soul of a leader is defined by how well these kinds of situations are handled. Often political shrewdness, compromise, negotiation, collaboration and other cooperative measures are necessary to effectively resolve these political issues which interfere with the decision-making process.

An educational example of this kind of situation might be the case of a marginal teacher who is not successfully teaching children. The teacher has to be dismissed because the children are not being taught. The leader may determine that dismissing the teacher is the right thing to do, but contract language between the teacher's union and school district prevents the dismissal of this teacher and specifies how this teacher is to be handled. There is a defined process to follow which allows this unsuccessful teacher to have a chance to correct the situation. This process will take additional time and involve an improvement plan with strategies, activities and recommendations. This is a typical "Right, but…" scenario. The language of a master contract or legal contract agreement between the Board of Education and a teacher's organization could create its own political web of problems. Life would be so simple if everything was clearly "Right" or "Wrong" and all parties involved agreed to the same standards of right and wrong, but leadership situations are often shades of gray. The leader's rope has to be extremely strong to support the leader's efforts in resolving these "Right, but…" situations.

2. The second political situation to examine is "The Godfather Situation." This example creates opportunities for the leader to make individuals "an offer they cannot refuse." This technique is a power-play and it commonly occurs when the leader has to exercise power in a direct manner without compromising. It is strategic and necessary. An example of this occurred in the movie, "The Godfather," when Don Vito Corleone's henchmen told the businessman, "We are going to make you an offer you cannot refuse." They proceeded to say that "Don Corleone will have your signature on the contract or your blood on the contract." There was no room for a third option and no room for compromise. Remember that the nature of politics is built on compromise, but every once in awhile there will be a "Godfather" situation.

President Ronald Reagan reached that point in dealing with the air traffic controllers. When they failed to reach a settlement, he destroyed their union by terminating their employment. It was a matter of national safety and the public trust. President Reagan placed the safety of travelers above the union rights of the air traffic controllers.

President John Kennedy reached that point in dealing with the Russian arms buildup in Cuba. As a result, he initiated a naval blockade with a Godfather stance that brought the United States very close to World War III. The President could not allow weapons of mass destruction to be deployed on an island or country so close to our shores. It was a matter of national security. It was non-negotiable and the classic "Godfather situation."

The Walt Disney Company gave the city of New York a "Godfather" ultimatum regarding the city's role in cleaning up the 42nd Street area before they would open the Disney Theatre. At the time the 42nd Street area was loaded with double X porn houses, loitering, street peddlers and high crime rates, Disney could not invest major dollars in family entertainment in this area. The city cleaned the area up.

The Godfather situation results when the leader draws the "line in the sand" and sets non-negotiable terms. Politics at the ultimatum stage places the leader on the line or as Ronald A. Heifetz, Harvard Professor in the Kennedy School of Government, calls it "The Razor's Edge." Using an ultimatum is always a tough place for the leader to be. It might be an interesting place for the leader to visit, but a leader cannot live or survive very long on the ultimatum edge. As a matter of fact, when a leader resorts to an ultimatum, politics are extremely limited. Ultimatums create too much tension, discord, anger and retribution. However, every leader will eventually find himself in a Godfather situation.

3. The third example of politics in tough situations is the "Don't Rock the Boat or Else Situation." This situation is created primarily by selfishness, greed, fear, anti-change forces and other politics. It is an example that threatens the serenity and peacefulness of the situation. A school district could be operating very successfully. Student achievement, on average, might be very good. The community is pleased and proud of the schools. It all seems to be going just fine. However, a closer look finds that the district's school boundaries are strangely drawn to achieve desegregation. The burden of the desegregation initiative is on the backs of the poorest students in the district. They are also minority students. The desegregation process is one way bussing of poor minority students out of their neighborhoods across the district to primarily upper income and majority neighborhoods. No upper income or majority child is bussed out of his neighborhood. The leader is confronted with budget concerns requiring a budget reduction. The leader has to find ways to cut the budget. After extended study and information

gathering, the leader discovers that a great deal of money could be saved by changing to neighborhood schools for all students or some two-way bussing in the central section of the district. The leader has to decide how important it is to make a traumatic change which saves money and compromises the desegregation pattern or to cut staff and increase class size across the district. The politics of this "Don't Rock the Boat or Else" scenario are huge. The leader's rope has to be very strong to guide him in this situation. It is a "lose-lose" situation and the leader's job could hang in the balance. Which course of action creates the least damage? Is saving money worth creating havoc and discord? Who are the ultimate losers in this matter? What is the leader's obligation to Equality? Equity? Adequacy?

These three examples are common challenging situations filled with political implications and potential problems. Politics are as much a part of leadership as decision making. They require the leader to have a strong rope. Politics force the leader to make connections, build coalitions, collaborate and share, communicate clearly and effectively, know the community and the powerful people and forces in it.

Richard Farson, psychologist, former CEO and colleague of Carl Rogers, says, "…every management act is a political act." He believes, "that every management act in someway redistributes or reinforces power." In his mind these are some examples of political acts: Hiring a woman as a secretary and a man as a management trainee; switching from employees to contract services; maintaining wage differentials between men and women; employing a relative; building handicapped access for workers; mandating a retirement age; employing a woman as high school principal; promoting African Americans and other minorities over their white counterparts. He warns us to beware of political discrimination. Most of these acts are well meaning. Farson says, "There is a history, for example, of legislation by male lawmakers to protect women in the workplace – preventing them from having to lift heavy packages, guaranteeing them coffee breaks, providing cots in their rest rooms, and making it illegal to require overtime work…but that very legislation has 'protected' women into second class status, many of them into poverty.

Even now, women make only 75 percent of the pay men get for the same work. They are systematically excluded from management roles because it has been difficult for managers to see how someone who has a cot in her restroom or cannot be worked overtime should be put in a leadership position."[3] Farson's example was focused on the private sector, but many areas of the public sector employ the same politics. Leaders have to protect themselves from these kinds of politics by using a rope of fairness, equity, sound judgment for objective decision making and strong consideration for the followers.

The Rope Metaphor

The excuse that "politics" cause some leaders to fail is a legitimate one, but politics are as close to leadership as eyes to a nose on a face. Leaders have to deal with politics because politics are a part of leadership.

The rope or vision/plan has to accommodate politics in order to reach its full potential. Politics impact the leader and the followers. When the leader extends the rope to the followers, he/she knows that together they can overcome the challenges and obstacles presented by politics if they just hold the rope, and if they just believe in the vision/plan.

For example, if the leader's and followers' vision/plan or rope is to build a new hospital for the community, they know that they will have to overcome the challenges of raising funds, getting the land, seeking variances and permits, finding the architect and contractor, and solving many other challenges. They must hold the rope through all the politics created by the need to build the hospital. If they hold the rope and work at the job, the hospital will become a reality

Summary

Leadership does not exist without politics. Politics force leaders to build connections, collaborations, partnerships, and coalitions with other people, organizations and power brokers. Politics requires the leader to effectively communicate with followers, associates, and the general public. Leaders have to protect themselves from unfair politics by using a rope (vision/plan) of fairness, equity, objective decision making, and sound judgment with strong consideration for the followers, customers, and associates.

In working with boards, leaders must be sure that board members are holding the rope and that there will be no surprises. Communication is the key strategy in preventing surprises. Too much information is better than too little information. Leaders should never assume what board members might do. Educating board members is a priority for leaders. All leaders will someday face three basic situations: (1) "The Right, but..." situation, (2) "The Godfather situation," and (3) "The Don't Rock the Boat or Else situation." Politics at the ultimatum stage of "The Godfather Situation" is a dangerous place to be. Ultimatums contradict the essence of politics, which is *the* compromise. Ultimatums create too much tension, discord, anger and retribution. And yet, every leader will eventually force a "Godfather" ultimatum. The wise leader must keep ultimatums to as few a number as possible.

References:

1. The Bible: The Book of Acts, Chapter 16:1-21.
2. Farson, R. (1996). Management of the absurd. New York:
   Simon & Schuster.
3. Ibid.

CHAPTER SIX

EXCUSE #4: MONEY

**"If I just had more money,
I would be a successful leader."**

"A Leader Will Never Have Enough Money"

Dr. Eugene G. White

The Money

A common reason given to excuse unsuccessful leadership is that "if I just had more money, I would be a successful leader. Money is seen as the "answer" to the leadership problems of the unsuccessful leader. They feel that if he/she just had enough money, all problems would be solved. Someone once said that throwing money at the problem might not solve it, but I would like to try it just once. Leaders fully understand that money sets things in motion and makes things happen, but a leader must have a plan in order to appropriately utilize the available money.

Not having enough money does not reduce the leader's responsibility to lead. The first step for a leader is to assess the current allocation of available funds. The leader should conduct an audit of revenue and expenses. Assuming that the current revenue is flat with little or no increase, the leader should develop a spending priority listing and justify all expenses.

Many leaders are surprised to find that they already have the funds available to make changes, implement different programs, buy additional advertising, or increase staff training. The leader must make the appropriate decision to optimize spending. At first glance, it may seem easy to save expenses by reducing staff or eliminating a division and exporting the work, but eliminating the followers to save money also has costs.

Once followers have taken the rope and are working to make the vision and plan a reality, separating them from the rope and the job destroys their trust and ownership in the organization. The leader must achieve the vision and plan and convince the remaining followers to hold the rope even tighter than before.

Leaders are responsible for making the available money go as far as possible. Leaders are expected to know how to generate money, invest money, spend money, and protect money. Therefore, one of the first acts a prospective leader should accomplish is to research the financial viability of the organization. Researching the financial viability of an organization should include asking the following questions:

1. What is the revenue source for the organization?
    -   Is it solid?
    -   What are some possible problems with the revenue source?
    -   How is the revenue source impacted by the economy?
    -   Are there additional sources of revenue?
2. What are the year end operating balances for the last five years?
    -   How is the operating balance defined?
    -   Are expenses exceeding revenue?
    -   When was the last year end deficit balance?
3. What is the greatest expense of the organization?
    -   Completely define the options for controlling or reducing expenses.
4. Can this organization financially support the prospective leader's vision and plan?

- What are its commitments to fund change?
- Who controls the organization and its dollars?
- Are the financial operations solid and well managed?

These four general questions will give the leader enough data to form a good picture of the financial status of the organization. Some leaders do not mind a tight financial situation because their vision and plan will generate greater revenue. Knowing the financial position of the company before a leader takes a job will result in more realistic expectations and a vision and plan which is tailored to the ability of the organization to sustain it.

Salary Issues

How the leader budgets the available funds can create problems for a leader if others see the leader as greedy or self serving. Leaders who work for boards have to establish solid communication about finances. These financial matters cover a wide range of circumstances. Financial considerations begin with salary and run through operational expenses.

I urge leaders to have a third party negotiate his/her salary with the board. This negotiation could include stocks, insurance, bonuses, performance incentives, and other fringe benefits. Involving an outside negotiator eliminates the picture of the leader making a case for his/her money. Good contracts eliminate many money problems between leaders and boards.

Once a contract is signed, the leader should honor the contract; however, most good contracts have "out" clauses or separation language to facilitate separation should one of the parties wish to end the agreement. Leaders cannot afford to take chances with their employment contracts. A leader should always seek good legal counsel and negotiate the best possible contract for both sides.

Money and Motivation

When working with followers or employees, leaders must remember that money satisfies and motivates at the lower and mid levels of personal needs, but it is not the ultimate motivator. The leader, his rope (vision/plan) and organization are the ultimate motivators. People give their lives for causes such as love of country, democracy, family, and religion. No amount of money can compensate for these causes.

In the period from the early 1950's through the 1970's large companies provided lifetime security and support for many employees. In this era people didn't readily change jobs. In Japan the company became the center of the workers' lives. They were loyal to companies and companies took care of them. The "company man" label applied to the relationship. This bond created a union or family stronger than money could buy. This relationship created a motivation just as strong or stronger than the motivation of salaries. Company loyalty was and is a strong motivator when the leader knows how to connect the worker with the company and vice versa.

Money can be part of the answer to motivate followers to connect with the leader and the rope, but money can never be the total answer. People seek associations and connections that money will not buy. Sharing ownership with them, involving them in decisions, respecting their opinions, celebrating their successes, helping them to learn more and improve, honestly assessing their performance, being there to relate to them, and other personal and caring practices will be just as important as money in building a successful team.

William F. Whyte, in his research on industrial relations, found that money is not as strong a motivational tool as many leaders are led to believe. This was especially true for production workers. When interviewed by Whyte's researchers, many of these workers placed the approval of the group above the motivation of money. They wanted to be accepted and approved by the group. Whyte estimated that only about 10 percent of the production workers in the United States would ignore group pressure and produce as much as possible in response to an incentive plan of more money. These workers valued their personal comfort on the job. They were concerned about enjoyment on the job and their long-range job security more than receiving extra money from an incentive plan.[1]

Leaders must find alternative ways to motivate people who have enough money. Job satisfaction, purpose, service, philosophy, history, legacy, tradition, faith, and many other things motivate people when money is not enough.

Leaders must remember that people do not take their money with them when they die. In life, money does not meet all one's needs. Comparing those who have little money vs. those who have much money is like comparing a good offensive football team with a good defensive football team. A good offensive player may run the ball well sometimes, but the good defensive team will not let that one player run it well all the time. A quarterback may pass the ball successfully sometimes, but the defensive team will not allow the quarterback to pass it successfully all the time. Using money for motivation is like the pass in football. It will work successfully one play, but may be totally ineffective the next. The leader must have another play to off-set the pass (a run). Life is like that tough defensive football team. Some circumstances will knock the leader down. A leader must have a plan to succeed. Using money to solve difficult circumstances will only work part of the time. For other times, the leader needs a strong rope to pull the team through difficult circumstances.

Professional athletes with money are often motivated by winning. After winning some games, they want to win the championship. If the championship is won, they want to defend it and win it again. Some people are motivated by being a part of something greater than they ever imagined; such as participation in an outstanding performing arts group, team, company, corporation, or church. Money is important, but leaders have to know how to motivate followers when money is not enough.

The Rope Metaphor

The excuse of not having enough money causing a leader

to fail is a common one. Money is an important tool contributing to a leader's success. Money enables leaders to do some very important things. However, money is not the ultimate motivator or the absolute answer to all leadership concerns.

Money can help the leader make great strides in achieving the vision/plan or rope, but the success of the leader's rope needs the support of followers. Money is not the ultimate motivator for people. Many professional sports teams are coming to the realization that money is not enough to make the team a winner. If the vision and plan for a team is to win the NBA championship, money will get the players, but it will not guarantee the championship. The ability to attract and pay for good players could improve the odds, but there are other variables needed for success that money cannot buy. The leader (coach, general manager, and owner) and the followers (players) must share the same rope or vision/plan. They have to hold that rope in season and out of season. They must hold the rope through good times and bad times. In addition to money, they must build trust, ownership and accountability. They have to create a will strong enough to hold the rope and believe in the rope until the championship is won.

In pro sports today it is hard to develop this kind of dedication to the rope or vision/plan for a team. The "business" of sports, including salary caps, forces players to drop ropes and pick-up new ropes too frequently. The desire to obtain more money creates disunity because it motivates players to move from team to team. Too many ropes or too many teams, results in too many visions and plans. This situation creates mercenary ball players loyal only to their agents and union representatives with no loyalty to vision.

Do the higher salaries paid by other teams cause the coaches or owners with less money to fail? No. There are many examples in high school, college and professional sports where the underdog over achieves and becomes successful. This is not to say that money doesn't play a big role in who wins and loses. Those teams which can afford to keep more great players in one place for years have the better chances of winning. However, as the L.A. Lakers found out in the 2003-2004 season money and talent do not guarantee a championship.

Money is important. Successful leaders have to find ways to control and utilize money and avoid being victimized or defeated by it. People are the ultimate key to success and leaders are wise to understand the different ways to motivate followers besides offering them more money.

Summary

Many leaders believe that money, primarily the lack of money, prevents them from achieving the success they want to achieve. Leaders must research the financial circumstances of an organization before taking on the job. They must answer four basic questions pertaining to money in order to generate a general understanding of an organization's financial situation: (1) What is the revenue source for the organization? (2) What are the year-end operating balances for the last five years? (3) What is the greatest expense of the organization? (4) Can the organization financially support your vision/plan?

There will never be enough money. The leader has to make the vision and plan happen anyway. The first step for a leader in a new job is to ascertain the expenses and current cash flow. The leader must conduct an audit of revenue and expenses and develop a spending priority listing which satisfactorily justifies all expenses. ***Leaders must control the money and not allow money to control them.*** Leaders who work with boards should employ an attorney or a third party to negotiate his/her contract. A good contract avoids money problems between leaders and boards.

Money is a motivator, but it motivates best at lower and mid levels of personal needs. It is not the ultimate motivator. It is not the total answer. People seek associations and connections that money will not buy. Sharing ownership, involving followers in decision-making, respecting their opinions, celebrating their successes, helping them to learn more and improve, honestly evaluating their work and being there to support them are just as motivating as money at higher levels of need. Industrial research by William F. Whyte validates the power of the group as a motivator compared to the incentive of more work for more money. Effective leaders understand that money is an important motivator, but know how to motivate followers when the money is not enough to get the job done.

References:

1. Whyte, W. F. (1955). <u>Money and motivation</u>. New
   York: Harper & Row, Publishers.

CHAPTER SEVEN

EXCUSE # 5: TIME

**"If I just had more time,
I would be a successful leader."**

"Time cannot be borrowed, stored, or recycled; it can only be spent as it is received, twenty-four hours in each day. Thus, time management means self management, managing oneself with respect to a non controllable resource"

Dr. Ivan Fitzwater

TIME

One of the most frequently stated reasons for lack of leadership success is "If only I had more time, I would be a successful leader." Some common statements are: "If I had been given just a little more time to get it done, I would have finished!"; "I couldn't control the time needed to get it done."; "How could they expect me to do it in such a short period of time?" The complaints are endless, but the bottom line is always the same; there is enough time to succeed. Unsuccessful efforts, projects, campaigns, or programs don't succeed because of a lack of time, but more often from a lack of effective leadership or a lack of effort.

I must be fair with this excuse because there are some situations where time is blamed for the failure, but no amount of time could solve the problem. However, in most cases time becomes the excuse because it is such an easy excuse to make. How can one control time? If time is running against a leader, the situation is daunting. In reality, we will never have enough time to do all we want to do. All leaders confront the realities and limits of time.

Dr. Ivan Fitzwater, a leading expert in time management for school administrators, said, "Time cannot be borrowed, stored, or recycled; it can only be spent as it is received, twenty-four hours in each day. Thus, time management means self management; managing oneself with respect to a non-controllable resource."[1] The best defense against a lack of time is good planning. Leaders have to take control of their lives and make appropriate plans to maximize time. With leaders and time, the most important feature is planning, planning and planning! Fitzwater said, "Failure to organize causes expansion of the time required to do a task, induces uncertainty through lack of purpose and permits a crisis atmosphere to prevail."[2]

A leader has to organize and prioritize those tasks which need to be accomplished. It is hard to lead when a lack of time makes a leader feel out of control of the situation. The leader who fails to plan, plans to fail. Doing something as simple as making a daily list of things to do makes a leader more effective. A "to do list" eliminates procrastination and focuses the leader. The time needed to get the job done is greatly reduced when planning comes first. The concept of plan, act, and evaluate (PAE) is a valuable time saving process for leaders.

A leader has to define what is urgent and what is not urgent, what is important to do and what is not important to do. The leader must identify what is truly an emergency and what is not an emergency. Once a leader chooses the priorities, he/she must act within the time frame they have to see that the tasks are accomplished.

Time: The Dependency Trap

In an article by Marshall Goldsmith in the June 2004 issue of the "Fast Company" called "Get-Out-Of-My-Face-Time," the author shares the story of an editor-in-chief of one of the top women's magazines who is very dedicated and a well-organized leader. This editor took pride in her ability to juggle a high-pressure job and maintain a sane personal life with her husband and two young children. She always tried to be home by 6:30 each evening to spend time with her children. She was considered a great boss by her staff. She was an excellent listener and she had a practice of keeping her door open to everyone. As a result of this openness, many of her employees started to bring more and more issues to her for a reaction or an approval. She found herself making more and more excuses for working late. Soon she was regularly at her desk until 9:30-10:00 p.m. She thought, initially, that this was happening because she really valued and loved her job. But she soon started to realize that these late evenings had nothing to do with her love for her work. Her good start as an effective leader and time manager had been eroded when she allowed her staff to depend on her too much.[3]

One of the potential down sides of being in a power position is creating dependency. Leaders should clearly know and understand how much they depend on people in their organization and conversely, how much people in their organization depend on them. Leaders should help, support, nurture and direct their employees, but they should be constantly educating and preparing their followers to assume more ownership and responsibility for doing their jobs. Leaders must understand that the more they are respected and admired by the staff, the more the staff may feel the need to gain their approval. Goldsmith went on to say, "...if their leader chooses to spend her limited time with any one person, that person's ideas and opinions must be uniquely valued. This usually plays out as a grab for face time with the manager. The editor finally had to tell her employees that face time had to end at 5:45 p.m.; however, reverting to her previous end of work boundary did not work because her staff was now hooked on seeing her for approval. Her staff perceived this new boundary as punishing them for a situation she created."[4]

Open door policies are great, and being engaged and supportive of staff is recommended, but the leader must also protect time to get his/her job done. There is a saying common in the business world which goes, people by day, paper by night. This simply means that leaders who spend their time with people during the day will have to spend their time doing their paperwork at the end of the day after the people have left to go home. When leaders are fully involved with their staffs during the day, some reading, thinking and administrative activities will be delayed. Leaders have to prioritize their activities and complete the essential tasks. An effective leader will utilize delegation and find other ways to involve followers in getting the job done. Nevertheless, there are some things that leaders have to do. Make sure to identify these "must do" things and accomplish them.

Leaders have to protect themselves from the time trap of dependency. The dependency trap cuts both ways; the followers need to depend on the leader and the leader needs to feel important and needed by the followers. In either case dependency takes valuable time from the leader. Dr. R. Alec MacKenzie called employees' dependency "Reverse Delegation." He said that there are at least six reasons for reverse delegation:

1.   The subordinate wishes to avoid risk.

2.   The subordinate is afraid of criticism.

3.   The subordinate lacks confidence which comes from experience and knowledge.

4.   The subordinate lacks the necessary information and resources to accomplish the job successfully.

5.   The boss wants to be needed.

6.   The boss is unable to say no to requests for help.[5]

No matter what the reasons for employees taking up to much of the leaders time, the reasons must be dealt with quickly and consistently. The job of the leader is too complex to allow time to be wasted. Time is a valuable resource that cannot be replenished.

Time Wasters

Dr. Ivan Fitzwater did some valuable work in analyzing how leaders waste time.   Dr. Fitzwater said that there are basically two groups of time wasters, The Internal Time Wasters and the External Time Wasters.   The Internal Time Wasters are: Lack of Delegation, Fire Fighting, Lack of Plans, Lack of Priorities, Open Door Policy, and Procrastination. The External Time Wasters Are: Telephone, Meetings, Visitors, Paperwork, and Delays. Dr. Fitzwater believes that time wasters are essentially the same for all busy people and that once identified they can be eliminated or at least controlled.[6]

Of these time wasters identified by Dr. Fitzwater, there are five that stand out and deserve further discussion.

In either case it is the leader who must control their time in how it is spent in the most productive manner possible. Especially when a leader becomes successful in an organization it is easy to become involved in too many activities or too many commitments. Being overly involved prevents leaders from having enough time to do any of the activities or commitments very well. This predicament of being over committed often comes from the inability to say "No." However, it could result from the leader's desire to provide services to his/her profession or community. Regardless of the cause, the results seriously compromise the leader's available time. Leaders have to selectively choose what is required to do; what is important to do; what is optional to do; and what is not worth doing. Leaders have to prioritize their time by prioritizing their activities and schedule. A balance of family, profession, and service must always be the goal. Over emphasis in any of these would adversely affect the person in the organization they are trying to lead.

Delegation

One way to see that this balance is acheived is through delegation. With only so many hours in the day and with a myriad of tasks to be completed, an effective leader needs to be able to delegate within the organization. Some leaders are reluctant to delegate authority because they fear losing control. Some leaders try to do everything because they do not trust others to do it the "right" way. Some leaders fear delegation because they have failed to prepare others to lead. Leaders should not assign tasks to others until they are assured that the designee can do the job. Leaders should not assume that others know what to do, but they must actively prepare others to assume leadership. Leaders should educate and elevate their assistants. This will create more leaders and save time for the leader.

Marshall G. Bryant said, "When your love of authority exceeds your sense of responsibility, your leadership is in jeopardy and so is the organization you lead." The reward for expanding leadership is an added opportunity to better use time. Leaders can delegate authority to others to complete an assignment, and need to trust it will be done properly.[7]

Meetings

Another major time waster is meetings. Most people would agree there are just too many of them. However, meetings can be timely, concise, well organized and short. Meeting time can be time well spent. Leaders can use meetings to have a tremendous impact on the morale, productivity, and culture of an organization. A bad meeting could be a negative reflection on the organization. Leaders value employees' time because it is a valuable resource. But the negative impact of a meeting can be more important than the lost productivity that a meeting creates. Bad meetings impact the attitudes of the attendees. Meetings should be organized group communication sessions. Leaders want the message to be positively received and that fact alone demonstrates the value of having a good meeting.

A meeting should start on time because it is disrespectful to have people wait for those who failed to be prompt. If late comers are allowed to show up late with no consequences, those who are prompt will start to come late. Leaders must set a tone for promptness by starting on time and they must deal with people who are late for meetings. Leaders should start meetings on time and do everything possible to end meetings on time as a matter of respect to their followers.

Every meeting should have an agenda. The agenda is the road map for the meeting. A consent agenda allows the leader to send out written materials containing announcements that do not require discussion, prior to the meeting. The leader sets the tone for meetings in the organization. If meetings are important, the way they are conducted and the outcomes should be evident to those asked to attend.

The following ten recommendations make meetings more efficient and relevant:

1. Send an agenda in advance with a starting and ending time
2. Invite the right people to attend
3. Make all preparations for the meeting before the meeting
4. Start on time, do not make people wait

5.   Do not repeat anything for late comers

6.   Review the purpose of the meeting at the beginning

7.   Do not deviate from the meeting agenda

8.   Control the meeting

9.   Summarize results when possible and thank people for coming

10.   End on time

Meetings are a good way to effectively communicate to groups of followers or employees. The leader must make effective use of the time spent in meetings.

Another time waster is the telephone. If utilized properly, the telephone can be a time saver. It can prevent meetings and time needed to get to them. A conference call can bring many people together to discuss issues without leaving their offices. This also saves multiple calls. A phone saves useless trips. It saves writing letters or sending e-mails. However, as good as the phone is for saving time, it also has the potential for wasting time. Some leaders get involved in more issues because of the telephone. A tendency to talk too long on calls takes away valuable time, especially if the recipient does not know how to say goodbye when the purpose of the call has been accomplished.

Failure to have calls screened creates problems, especially leaders who fail to educate their secretaries or assistants to screen calls. It is estimated that most leaders spend at least an hour on the phone each day. There is a need for telephone discipline. Just because someone calls doesn't mean the task or the person being dealt with should become secondary to the phone call.

Good secretaries and assistants are valuable if they can facilitate and control the incoming calls for the leader. The leader has to have an assistant who is skillful at answering incoming calls. The person must be trained to ascertain the urgency and needs of the caller and connect the caller to the appropriate designee. This assistant should be trained to protect the time of the leader. The person will have to know others in the organization who can answer or respond to the caller and be able to delegate calls to these people. For calls only the leader can answer, the assistant must ascertain the urgency of the call. If the call is urgent, but not an emergency, the assistant should know the appropriate response. Protecting the time of the leader is an appropriate job expectation and should be delegated to the assistant.

In addition to assistants, other technologies such as call back systems, and voice mail are available to help deal with telephone distractions. The leader must utilize a good assistant and electronic call-back systems in order to deal with the demands of the telephone.

Technology such as the computer and e-mail were created to simplify the lives of leaders. Supposedly, these technologies were going to save time. Communication, research, and clerical functions have been greatly enhanced by the computer, but it can become as big a time waster as the telephone. Computers can be addicting. The more one uses them, the more one finds needs to use them. E-mail can free up time for leaders if appropriate delegations and strategies are in place. A good strategy for email is to have it come through an assistant for screening. This eliminates hours of deletions and trivial messages. Leaders should seek ways to prevent the waste of time through the use of electronic technology and communication.

Leaders have to demonstrate self-discipline in eliminating invasions on their time. Time is commonly wasted by failing to get started. Norman Vincent Peale, author and renowned positive thinker, had serious problems with procrastination until he faced up to it. Here are his simple guidelines against procrastination:

1. Pick one area where procrastination is a problem and conquer it.
2. Learn to set priorities and focus on one problem at a time.
3. Give yourself deadlines.
4. Do not duck the most difficult problems.
5. Do not let perfectionism paralyze you.[8]

Eliminating procrastination starts with the leader. Leaders need to make a decision, dispose of papers, deal with reports, meet with people, face negative situations, write the report, or take the necessary actions needed to get things going. The leader should push to "Do it now!" Leaders must act!!

Leaders can deal with huge problems by breaking them into doable pieces, taking them one piece after the other until the problem is solved. As is true in the solution of other time wasters, planning helps to attack procrastination. Leaders must attack procrastination by planning, acting and evaluating the results. Dr. Mackenzie, noted expert on time management said,

> The ability to concentrate – to persevere on a course without distraction or diversion is a power that has enabled men of moderate capabilities to reach heights of attainment that have eluded the genius. They have no secret formula other than to persevere. Such men must have learned their limitations early, and they must have learned also that concentrated effort over a protracted period can be more productive than a momentary flash of genius. They are unlikely to succumb to that hidden but insidious time waster, the habit of leaving tasks unfinished.[9]

The Rope Metaphor for Time

A key to successful and effective leadership is to get the followers to embrace the rope of the leader. The leader has to use time to ensure success. Followers have to fully understand the role they play in its success. They cannot waste time or opportunities. They cannot be late or disconnected. They have to be there with the rope. The followers must accept the responsibility for acting. They have to implement and achieve the vision.

The leader wants followers who are willing to accept delegation. Through these tasks and assignments new leaders are created. The rope can be longer with more leaders taking ownership. The leader gives followers the authority to lead and sets expectations for the overall success of the organization.

Summary

One of the most frequent excuses for failed leadership is "time." There is never enough time, but leaders must still achieve their vision and plan in the time available. Time or lack of it is not an acceptable reason for failure.

Leaders have to be careful to avoid the trap of dependency. Dependency cuts both ways: The followers' need to depend on the leader and the leader's need to feel important and needed by the followers. In either case, dependency wastes the valuable time of the leader. Leaders must be aware of "reverse delegation." Followers want to avoid risk, blame, and responsibility and the leader helps them by making all their decisions or providing too much input.

Leaders have to utilize delegation to save time and to train future leaders. Some leaders are reluctant to delegate authority because they fear losing control; others want to do things the "right" way; still others fail to prepare followers to assume tasks or assignments. Leaders must learn to delegate and spend the valuable resource of time wisely.

The leader's success depends on followers who understand the vision and plan and accept the authority for acting. There is no room for procrastination. Delegation is very important for building new leaders and greater ownership for the rope.

References:

1. Fitzwater, I. Dr. (1996). Time management for school administrators. Rockport, Massachusetts: Pro>Active Publications.
2. Fitzwater, I. Dr. (1996). Time management for school administrators. Rockport, Massachusetts: Pro>Active Publications.
3. Goldsmith, M. Get-out-of-my-face-time. Fast Company. June 2004.
4. Ibid.
5. MacKenzie, R. A. (1972). The time trap. New York, N.Y.: Amacom, American Management Association, Inc.
6. Fitzwater, I. Dr. (1996). Time management for school administrators. Rockport, Massachusetts: Pro>Active Publications.
7. MacKenzie, R. A. (1972). The time trap. New York, N.Y.: Amacom, American Management Association, Inc.
8. MacKenzie, R. A. (1972). The time trap. New York, N.Y.: Amacom, American Management Association, Inc.

CHAPTER EIGHT

EXCUSE #6: SYSTEM

**"If the system would work more smoothly,
I would be a successful leader."**

"Working as a team is not about liking people. You just need
to stick together – to respect diversity, to realize that everybody
adds value, and to understand the goal."

Dean Hohl

THE SYSTEM

I have been doing a great deal of flying recently and as I fly and observe the operations of the different airlines, I realize that many of my thoughts on systems are exemplified by the airline industry. The airline is an example of an organization whose goal and mission depends on the systems employed by the company for success. The mission of most airlines is to provide safe, affordable air travel to the general public to as many destinations as possible. The airline's goal is to make money and turn a profit for its shareholders. The systems of the airplane operation will determine the success or failure of the mission. The customer service system starts the process and the systems continue through the flight itself, to the baggage pick-up at the destination. Every system involving a flight depends on people to make it successful.

If a new chief executive officer took control of an airline company and wanted to make it more cost efficient, provide better service, safer flights, and increased customer satisfaction, he/she would have to deal with one or more of these systems. In dealing with these systems, the CEO would have to work with pilot unions, mechanic or service unions, flight attendant's unions, etc. If the CEO found it tough or nearly impossible to work with the people of the systems, it would be understandable to hear this CEO say that the "system" is the problem. Nonetheless, it will be necessary for the CEO to work successfully with these entities to get the job done. It is common for leaders to lament about the system and the many obstructions and dysfunctional variables created by poor systems.

The system is a common term utilized by many people, but very few people understand the power or impact of a system on the success or failure of the people working in the organization. The leader is responsible for the system, but the leader does not own the system. It is important for the leader as well as other stake holders to understand that most issues are about problems not people. The first inclination when issues arise is to look to people to blame rather than looking for a problem to solve. The system should be examined before the person is blamed.

Leaders commonly make the error of reacting to or over reacting when they focus the attention of one of their followers or workers on any mistake or problem without first ascertaining if the assigned follower was actually responsible for the problem. The leader needs to find out if the follower made the mistake or if the problem was caused by the system. A leader cannot answer what he/she does not know. This is why education, training and experience are so important. If one is driving down the road and the car stops running, the driver must be sure to check how much gas is in the car before dismantling the engine. If the driver does not know what gasoline does to fuel the engine system, the driver could be dismantling the malfunctioning car (effect) and missing the cause (no gas in the engine). In the final analysis, the real problem could be the driver and not the car. If the driver fails to put gas in the car, the automotive system is not to blame. Successful and effective leaders must know how to check the gas gauge before they open the hood of the organization.

These two errors of leadership: assigning system

problems to other causes (special cause) and assigning problems in other causes to the system (common cause) have resulted in numerous mistakes, findings, loss of productivity, jobs, careers, and organizations. Leaders should avoid these two mistakes. However, many leaders avoid mistake number one by making mistake number two. Others avoid mistake number two by making mistake number one. Leaders have to understand that the action required to find and eliminate a special cause problem is different from the action required to improve the process. Leaders have to search for the special cause of a problem as soon as possible and once it is found, they must take the appropriate action. It might not be possible to completely eliminate the cause, but a process has to be initiated to reduce its impact or variation.

It is dangerous to utilize personal judgment to distinguish between special cause problems and common cause problems. The leader has to develop a means to generate or ascertain enough data or information to make a decision. Using surveys, interviews, meetings, observations, research and expert consultations can help in matters pertaining to people, organization structures, or planning.

A Look at Systems:

There are systems at work all around us. Notice the systems of the body: The digestive system, the reproductive system, the nervous system, the respiratory system, the endocrine system and the circulatory system. All the systems depend on various parts to keep functioning. The system is just as strong as its weakest part. Organizations have similar systems and it is essential that followers know the purpose of the system and what role their part or group plays in it. They should understand how their efforts can improve the system and conversely how the system impacts their efforts. Everything is connected in the system and every part is related to every other part in some manner. A dysfunctional part can cause other parts to over compensate to correct the problem. This overcompensation can create bigger problems for the system.

Systems problems involving human dynamics and social interactions are the toughest to solve. Leaders understand that one answer will not fit all problems. Understanding people and their needs is a solid starting point for leaders. People who understand the system and their roles in it are prepared to help improve the system. It is the leader's responsibility to define the system, the parts, and the roles in it. The leader has to work with others to improve. The common excuse that the system is preventing the leader from doing the job is real, but it is not acceptable. The system has to be corrected.

It seems that the larger the organization or company, the more complex the systems. This appears to be true when we look at the entire organization, but focusing on the core or heart of the entity reduces the complexity. Delta Airlines is a large, complex organization with multiple systems in place, but its core is a focus on service, safety, and profit. Its accountability measures focus on standards to keep it in business and make returns on investments. The CEO has to make sure all the parts and people work together to achieve success and effectiveness.

It is possible to have the best car parts in the world: the best fuel injection system, the best tires, the best spark plugs, the best engine, and still have a car which does not run well. Likewise, and organization can employ the best and the brightest managers and still be a mediocre operation. Within a system, it is possible to have the sum equal less than the parts, or conversely, to have the synergy of the sum being greater than its parts. The key is how things work together to make the system successful. The parts or people have to be optimized to work with each other toward a common goal or outcome. A leader's job is to see that everyone in the system works together to make the system a valuable part of the organization or company. The leader's vision is the common connection to all parts of the system and all systems in the organization.

When followers and workers see the system as "everything else but them," the leader's rope has failed to connect them to the system of the organization. They have no understanding of the role they play in making the system work. They have not been educated to take ownership for their part of the system's success. In a broader sense, they really do not know about the organization or its purpose. The organization has compromised its effectiveness and productivity by failing to connect the follower to the system. The effective leader will not allow followers to be disconnected from the system. This disconnect would result in a waste of talent and productivity. Followers have a great deal to add to the success of a system and organization. Their talents and expertise have to become a part of the system.

Leaders can improve systems and their effectiveness by following these ten recommendations:

1. Ensure that all followers or workers understand the organization and the systems of the organization.

2. Clearly define the roles of followers or workers in the organization and systems of the organization.

3. Ensure that followers and workers know the vision of the organization and the plan for achieving the vision. Work to create a community of believers.

4. Initiate a staff development program to train followers to improve their performance and the productivity of the organization.

5. Create a process to involve followers in problem solving, decision making and discussions pertaining to their areas of training, knowledge and expertise.

6. Establish performance benchmarks for each part of the system and set assessment time frames for review.

7. Create quality assurance committees to improve system practices, products and operations.

8. Ensure quality communication in the system and within the organization. The motto of "no

surprises" should guide the communication efforts.

9.   Create a process of people, system and organizational evaluation and improvement.

10.   Initiate a program of recognition, celebration and reward for outstanding achievement.

The Rope Metaphor

Blaming the system as an excuse for leadership failure is an excellent opportunity to examine how having the courage to hold the rope can correct this problem. The leader's rope is the guiding connection that holds the systems and organization together. The rope provides the common thread that should touch each follower.

The followers will not connect to the system unless they understand their role or place in it. They will hold the rope of the system when they understand and own it. It is the leader's job to make sure that followers know what is expected of them and what value they will receive from their participation. The leader might have to extend a short rope to followers initially, but through education, training, involvement, opportunities to serve and shared input, the followers will take a greater interest and more ownership in the rope.

Followers should be going in the same direction with the rope and the leader. There is no need for a 'tug-of-war" over the rope. The leader uses the rope to improve the system and the organization.

For the purposes of illustration, assume that the system is a heavy block of cement which has to be placed in the bed of a pick-up truck. The pick-up truck is the organization and it needs this system (the heavy block of cement) in place in order to move forward. The leader, or truck driver, needs a tool to give to the workers to help them put the system (block of cement) in place in the organization (truck). The leader gives the workers the vision: "We have to move this organization forward and we need this system in place to get the organization to Indianapolis." The leader gives them a plan: "We have to pull this cement block up the incline into the bed of the truck, and into the proper place for the organization to succeed." The leader teaches the followers their role: "You can make this happen and I cannot move this truck forward without you. You are the most important part of the organization and we cannot get to Indianapolis without you." The leader provides education, training and encouragement to the followers on ways to use a rope to pull a heavy object and how to secure it in place once it is in the proper position.

The leader's mental rope here is the vision of what the system (the cement block) is and its place in the organization (truck) and where the organization needs to go (Indianapolis). The plan involves how the block can be put in place on the truck. The training and education in the use of the rope to move the cement block (system) into the bed of the truck (organization) make the followers more aware of their roles. However, the most powerful rope could be the workers' view of their role in making the vision come true.

The followers know what the organization is and they

know the role of the system. They know what they have to do to move the system in place or where it should be in the organization. They are fully connected to the system. They understand the importance of the rope in moving the system and they know the rope is no good without their help. They also know the organization cannot move forward successfully without their involvement. The leader has to also hold that rope with them to get the job done. The leader, the rope, and the workers have a common vision and plan for success. The organization will benefit from this collaboration.

The leader wants followers to say, "This is our rope." When followers take ownership for the rope or system and understand that they can participate in changes to it and improving it, new leaders start to emerge. They can now extend the rope for others to hold. Success in system change and success in followers holding the rope both result in an increased number of leaders. System change is possible and leaders know that it all starts with a change in the awareness, knowledge, involvement and ownership of the followers. Holding the rope and working in a system has to be a learning opportunity. This adds value to the experience and enhances participation.

Summary

The excuse of the system preventing successful leadership is not a simple one to understand. The concept of "system" is somewhat amorphous. Many people have a very limited understanding of a system. There are systems all around us i.e.

nature systems, human systems, mechanical systems, electrical systems and technology systems. The leader is responsible for the organization, operation, upkeep and evaluation of the systems in an organization. People are the key to system improvement and productivity. Leaders have to connect workers to the system and organization. When workers see the system as "everything but us" it is a clear indication of a disconnect. Leaders must ensure that workers understand the organization, the systems, and their place in them. They have to know how they impact the system and why the system is good for them. They have to hold the system rope and know why it is important for them. There are ten recommendations to help leaders improve the system and organization.

The rope metaphor is closely aligned with the system problem. The leader's vision must be understood by followers if they are to become strong believers and possible future leaders. Educating and involving them in the vision and plan builds strong connections and ownership. Systems need leaders to take the same approach with workers. The system has to be a learning organization. This will add value and growth to the system. Systems are only as strong as their weakest part. Leaders have to ensure that all parts of the system are strong.

CHAPTER NINE

EXCUSE #7: COMPETITION

"If only I didn't have so much competition, I could be a successful leader."

"The spirit, the will to win, and the will to excel are the things that endure."

Vince Lombardi

COMPETITION

A common excuse given by some leaders is that the competition is interfering with the leader's ability to be a success. Leaders make various complaints about their adversaries such as: the competition is too rich, too powerful, too influential, too strong, too connected, too advanced, too smart, too big, too unfair, too this, or too that. All excuses connected to competition are generated from a lack of confidence on the part of the leader. The leader simply does not believe that his/her organization can compete with other organizations. There might be legitimate reasons for the leader to take the position that the competition is too good; however, to be successful, the leader must believe that through his/her vision and plan, the organization will be able to compete and achieve at or above the level of the competition.

Jeffrey Immelt, the CEO of General Electric, overcame a nightmare to turn his division around and head the company. In 1994, his division lost $50 million and his boss threatened to fire him. Immelt answered bluntly: "Look, if the results aren't what they should be, you won't have to fire me because I'm going to leave on my own." That commitment helped Immelt to turn his division around and take it to the top of the company. Immelt's attitude and will to turn his division around left no room for defeat. He gave his full commitment to overcome the loss.

One of the major factors in dealing with competition is to concentrate on one's vision and plan. A leader cannot lose sight of the goal by researching and looking at others. It is important to know the market, the environment, and the customers, but a leader's major time and effort has to be spent on his or her own operations and people.

When a leader accepts the challenge of competing with others, the leader would be wise to reflect upon the scene from the movie, The Empire Strikes Back. The future champion of the freedom fighters, Luke Skywalker, crashes his spacecraft into a swamp. His spiritual guide, Yoda, urges him to trust his instincts and his heart in the seemingly impossible task of levitating the craft from the murky water.

Luke, only half convinced says, "I'll try."

"No! Try not," says Yoda. "Do or do not! There is no try."

This non-compromising position is common among leaders who seriously want to compete in the market place. The leader has to believe his/her position to sell it to the followers. Most leaders fully understand that followers are watching them for directions and guidance. Followers believe in confident leaders acting on what they believe.

Competition demands that leaders commit to the moment. The vision and plan starts here and now. Lee Iacocca saved the Chrysler Automotive Corporation by turning the company around in its darkest hour. He became President of Chrysler in 1979 and quickly brought the company to a standard of efficiency and order. He reorganized the management of the company; implemented tight financial controls; improved quality control standards; changed the production schedule; and reduced staff to save money. He was tough with the unions, threatening to declare bankruptcy and put them out of work. Iacocca utilized a very short rope style of leadership with threats and mandates as its knots. He achieved outstanding results and Chrysler became one of the top turnaround stories in U.S. History. He took the company from near bankruptcy to nearly three times the general market. The success came not from looking at the competition for reasons they were failing, but looking within and establishing a plan to succeed.

My leadership experience taught me something about competition and turnaround in my first job as a high school principal at Wayne High School in Fort Wayne, Indiana. I had been an assistant principal there for three years. The varsity football team was unsuccessful; it was the product of a poorly operated football program. The head coach had solid knowledge of football theory and strategies, but he was weak in his ability to relate to young people. He had low expectations of the players individually and of them as a team. His assistant coaches were just as weak as he was and one of them told me that our boys could not win in football because they just were not good enough. He placed the responsibility for winning totally on the players. This was hard for me to accept because of the school's enrollment of more than 700 boys. Each year we lost to a team with half that number of boys. However, the team we lost to had an outstanding football coach. He was a teacher, coach and the athletic director. His name was Al Harants and he played football at Franklin College where he learned to play and coach the "Run-and-shoot" offense. His Bellmont teams often beat us with half the number of boys and less than half the number of coaches. After watching Coach Harants coach boys, I knew he could get our boys to win. There was an attitude and spirit in his program that was clearly missing in ours. Here's an example of how competition can be used as a catalyst for success rather than a reason for failure.

In the 1985 football season, we won one or two football games, but it turned out to be a great season because the coach resigned. My athletic director, Gary Patterson, invited Al Harants to apply for the job. We conducted a comprehensive interview process, but there was little doubt that Harants was the best candidate for the job. We employed Al Harants and in his first year, we won several football games and people could see that there was something different about our players. They now played with pride and positive attitudes. In Harants's second year as football coach, we won a football sectional and regional championship and lost a close game in the semi-state contest in Hobart, Indiana.

In the span of two years, a new football coach took us from last place in the conference to one game from the state championship. The boys were basically the same--they were from the same neighborhoods and communities as our previous teams. We did not give Harants more money or more assistant coaches than had been given to the previous coach. What enabled Harants to take an unsuccessful program from 'worst to first" in two years was his totally different approach to the students and their parents. His expectations were higher for each individual and the team. He had a clear vision and plan. He knew that football games are won in the off season and in the weight room. He saw the job of football coach at Wayne High School as a great opportunity to make his dreams come true. Coaching was not just a job with him, it was a passion. Coaching was not routine, it was special! He connected the dots by creating a system where every part of the process was important. Each of his players knew what he had to do to make the team a winner. Harants approached competition from the "inside-out." Harants knew his job thoroughly and was in control of his team. He expected them to perform with excellence, and they did. He studied the competition, learned from them and planned what he had to do to compete.

Al Harants's approach to competition in football at Wayne High School was like Jeffrey Immelt's approach to competition when he headed a division at General Electric; like Lee Iacocca's approach at Chrysler; like Vince Lombardi's approach with the Green Bay Packers; like Bill Parcells's approach with the New York Jets and the Dallas Cowboys; like the approach of Gary Williams with the University of Maryland's basketball program; and many other worst to first success stories. In observing these situations, I have identified seven basic things that successful leaders do when they take over losing or underperforming programs, organizations, or campaigns:

1. They have a vision/plan (rope) to turn around the low performing or unsuccessful program, organization or campaign. They clearly see positive outcomes and possibilities.

2. They demonstrate confidence in their ability to be successful through their communications and

actions. They leave little doubt that they can turn the program around.

3.   They clearly and effectively communicate their ideas, vision/plan, and expectations to peers, colleagues, followers and stakeholders.

4.   They make few, if any assumptions about what people already know. They assess and evaluate the current conditions of the organization to ascertain the true identity, characteristics, etc. They often use strategies and activities that involve people from the organization in the assessment process.

5.   They demonstrate skills, expertise, knowledge and talent to lead and influence the behavior of people. Some leaders utilize authoritative or "short rope" methods to get to know, orientate, in-service, and train employees or followers. Other leaders are less aggressive and employ collaborative orientation activities, training and in-service practices.

6.   They demonstrate the flexibility to use situational leadership strategies which are dictated by the task or challenge at hand.

7.   They understand and employ systemic change in the organization. They know that the system is no stronger than its weakest part and that all parts of the system have to be connected to create organization synergy.

The First Competition

Leaders who compete for success, effectiveness and victory understand that the toughest challenge is to get followers or employees to eliminate their common failures, excuses and limitations. No one truly competes against others before competing with him/her self. Each person needs to win his or her own personal battles before competing with others. If that battle isn't won the person will have to compete against self and the other competition. One has to be prepared to compete and self preparation is the first true competition. One has to be prepared by eliminating self-defeating practices, traditions, habits, systems, and cultures.

Texas Tech's new basketball coach Bob Knight turned around a low performing basketball program at Indiana University and won three national championships. Before Indiana he completely transformed a losing program at Army (Military Academy at West Point) and made it a winner. Now he has led the Texas Tech Program to victory. Coach Knight once said that, "everybody wants to win, but few are willing to prepare to win." He believes the winning is in the preparation. Coach Knight is right. The key to competing is in proper preparation for competition. Many want to compete but few are willing to properly prepare.

I read that a car maker was concerned with the number of new cars arriving at dealers with small scratches on the front panels or sides. There was a problem somewhere in the production process. The company conducted quality checks in the paint areas and found no problem. As the examiners walked the cars through the preparation process, they found the problem in the finishing area. In the finishing area, the workers had to make an adjustment in the windshield area of the car and their belt buckles were rubbing against the paint on the side of the cars. The belt buckles were creating the scratches.

Leaders have to be just as vigilant as the quality assurance workers at the car production facility. Leaders must seek out the causes of poor preparation. The causes of being unprepared are just like scratches on new cars. These flaws compromise the value of the product; and the readiness of the organization for competition.

From an accountability point of view, competition starts and ends with the leader. There is no competition if the leader does not want to have the best product, or have the best show, or have the best clothes, or have the best company, or have the most profit, or have the best record, or have the best team. Competition is born or created out of a desire to be the best or have the best. Competition is an internal drive. It is greatly influenced by external motivators and rewards.

Leaders are caught up in competition and its mandate because they are involved in activities, programs, productions, organizations, and politics that are judged and validated by their success against standards, expectations, profits, bottom lines, wins, productivity and other measures. However, leaders should not allow these external symbols of successful competition blind them to this primary truth: Competition is what the leader makes it. The questions and answers to winning competition start and end with people. Leaders who successfully influence, motivate and lead people will do a good job of competing. Competition does not cause leaders to fail. Systems cause leaders to fail. Leaders cause leaders to fail.

Rope Metaphor for Competition

The rope metaphor for competition is easy to picture. Preparing to compete is the ultimate competition. The leader sets the focus, effort and vision/plan for competition. The leader has to get followers to understand the value of eliminating self-defeating practices, habits, traditions, and cultures before they can expect to succeed.

The leader places the rope in the hands of followers by demonstrating the benefits of preparing for competition. Followers will not be able to hold the rope if they are not conditioned to do so. Followers need to learn ways to prepare to successfully hold the rope. When the weight of the challenge gets heavy, leaders and followers have to be mentally and physically strong enough to hold the rope. When the challenge is daunting and dangerous, the leader and followers have to demonstrate the courage to hold the rope. When the way is dark and forces mount against the effort, the leader and followers have to know how to stand and keep working for success. The vision/plan or rope prepares the leader and followers to compete.

Summary

Competition is sometimes blamed for causing some leaders to be unsuccessful. There is no doubt that competition can be challenging and difficult, but the leader has to create a vision/plan strong enough to deal with the competition. In order to compete, leaders must remember Yoda's words and "Do or do not!" There is no "Try." Followers are watching and could be "over the cliff" and need to be assured and confident of the strength of the rope they need the leader's vision/plan or "Rope" to hold. Competition demands that leaders commit to the moment. Leaders must get the job done now. Competition does not stand still and neither can the organization.

Successful leaders who have turned around under performing or unsuccessful programs seem to have many things in common. These leaders encourage their followers to win the first competition, which is the challenge of eliminating self-defeating practices, habits, traditions, systems, and cultures. The leader and followers will never be truly ready to compete against others until they master those things. Bob Knight was right, "everybody does want to win, but few are willing to prepare to win."

Leaders are caught up in competition's mandate because of the jobs they do or the roles they play. External validations and measures define who successfully competes. Successful leaders know that people decide how competitive an organization will be and that preparing to compete is the ultimate competition. Leaders who successfully and effectively influence, motivate and lead people will do a good job of competing. Competition does not cause leaders to fail. Leaders who fail to work successfully with their people will fail to be competitive.

CHAPTER TEN

EXCUSE #8: CHANGE

**"If only I didn't have to deal with change,
I could become a successful leader."**

"The urgent question of our time is whether we can make
change our friend and not our enemy."

President Bill Clinton

CHANGE

A final excuse for a lack of leadership success is change. Some leaders fail to adjust to the demands and expectations produced by change. Leaders approach change from four points of view. There is change created by the demands of the market place or environment; change that is created by legal mandates or laws; change created by the leaders and change created by the followers. Leaders must accept the fact that life is a sequence of changes. Everything will change. The most effective adjustment to change is created by the leaders and followers collaborating and taking ownership of the change. The leader's efforts to create change are the focus of this chapter. The leader has to work with change created anywhere in the organization and with changes from outside which impact the organization.

Dr. Douglas B. Reeves recently shared these myths and realities about change at the Indiana North Central Association Commission on Accreditation and School Improvement Annual Meeting:

Myth:	People are happy doing what they are doing now.
Reality:	People are miserable when they are not feeling successful in their professional lives, or when they fail to sense personal mastery.
Myth:	People resist change because of irrational fear.

Reality: People resist change because they have been burned before on changes that were poorly planned, badly executed, and resulted in more work for fewer results.

Myth: You can't make significant changes until you have buy-in from everybody.

Reality: Resistance to change is an organizational reality. The volume (noise) exceeds the volume (quantity) of the resistance.

Myth: You must have perfect research to support a proposed change.

Reality: Perfect research does not exist. Try it, test it, improve it, is far superior to waiting for the illusion of perfection. You need sufficient research and common sense.

Myth: The risk of change is so great that you must wait until you have things perfectly organized before implementing a change effort.

Reality: There is no risk-free alternative. The risks of change must be compared to the very significant risks of continuing current practices.

Reeves believes that, "change is never convenient; change is never universally popular; change is never without opposition; change is never risk-free; and change never gets easier over time." Although Reeves was referring to educational changes, these principles are applicable to most professions and organizations. While all people understand and experience change, few openly welcome change. There is always some apprehension because people are not sure how the change will affect them. People remember the bad examples of change more than they recall the good examples of change. Leaders need research and data to make good decisions about change, but there are some changes that only common sense can guide. There will seldom be 100% support data for change. Change requires or demands some degree of risk on the part of the leaders and followers. Leaders sometimes have to demonstrate the courage to make changes when the risks are high.

There are two basic ways to examine the impact of change on leaders: Change created by the leader and change forced upon the leader.

1. Change Created by the Leader

    Reinhold Niebuhr once said, "Grant me the serenity to accept the things I cannot change, the courage to change the things I can, and the wisdom to know the difference." Every leader should be aware of those issues and politics that should not be changed. These issues and politics create tremendous backlash and negative reactions. Being right or doing the right thing is often not strong enough to resolve or correct the situation, and sometimes leaders must be prepared to make the major sacrifice of losing their job in order to make the necessary unpopular changes which will benefit the organization.

Some examples of issues in education which require leaders to be willing to lose their jobs in order to make necessary changes are closing schools and changing attendance boundary lines. Often, the larger the school, the greater the number of critics or protestors. High schools are greatly impacted because generations of graduates get upset when the boundaries change the landscape of the schools where they graduated. These graduates often come back years later to criticize the leaders who would advocate such changes.

Issues related to closing schools and changing boundaries create deep emotional reactions. Often logic and data are disregarded because mothers or entire families graduated from the high school being changed. Leaders sometimes leave the decision unmade with a need for change pitted against their desire to keep their jobs. This is why on matters of school closing and boundary changes, leaders often appoint volunteers to serve on a committee or taskforce to review the matter. The decision to act is not totally owned by the leaders if a taskforce or committee makes the appropriate recommendation for change. Many school superintendents have learned this lesson the hard way and some have lost their jobs in the process.

2. Change forced Upon a Leader

Sometimes change occurs in spite of the action or inaction of the leader. Change takes place in the marketplace, or society at large. For example, technology has revolutionized the marketplace in the 21st century. Offices which do not use the computer for word processing and data entry, or companies which do not utilize email and the internet to transmit communication have become dinosaurs—outdated and too slow to effectively compete.

Think of the force of changing technology in business today. Few companies exist today without the help and incorporation of modern technology. One cannot effectively do business with internal and external customers without technology. Leaders who fail to change to this new reality have dropped the rope of leadership. This is not a volunteered change. It is change created by the market place or environment. It is non-negotiable.

Throughout history leaders have had change imposed or forced upon them. Many would argue or debate the rationale behind President Abraham Lincoln's decision to fight in the civil war. Did he sign the Emancipation Proclamation because he really wanted freedom for slaves, or was he forced into the war and the emancipation of slaves by the economic and political pressures on the United States? Was he a leader forced to change the status quo? If he was caught in a "forced change" situation, he was not the first leader to be compromised in this way and he certainly will not be the last.

Many leaders accept changes forced upon them and use the changes to make their vision stronger and their plan better. Others strategically create change to improve operations and ensure more success. Leaders know that change is inevitable and make flexibility part of their vision. However, even with a healthy respect for change, some leaders struggle to keep up. They fail to filter out essential change from non-essential change. They give in to the hopelessness of the continuous onslaught of new changes, and seek shelter from the realty of it all. But there is no place to hide from change.

A good example of a changing industry is that of musicians. In the 1950s, consumers listened to their music on 45 records and turntable record players. Next, the recording industry started making long playing albums to play on record players. Then consumers listened to their music on reel-to-reel tapes, which evolved into 8-track recordings, and then to cassette tapes. Next, the technology for music pleasure changed to compact discs and the players which played these CDs, and now, in 2004, the latest trend is to listen to music on an I-Pod. While some consumers resisted this change and wanted to stop with record players and 45 records or cassette tapes, change and new technology has forced many to change their listening habits. Recording studios stopped making the records and cassettes, so consumers had to keep what they had or change to the new technology. The pressure to change is fueled by the elimination of old technology. For leaders, the pressure to change is often fueled by the elimination of old choices.

Implementing Change

Leaders have to utilize change to improve the success and effectiveness of their organizations. Change will happen; therefore, leaders have to be able to identify the signs and indicators of change and get ahead of the action. To get ahead, leaders must develop plans and strategies to maximize change.

In order to diagnose, plan, strategize and control change, leaders have to have a comprehensive knowledge of their organization and its operations. Change will produce multiple benefits when leaders know how they must successfully interface with their organizational operations. Organizations have to be able to adapt to take advantage of change. Leaders have to have the flexibility to adapt their styles to accommodate the organizational change.

To be able to adapt to change, organizations must have employees who are able to acquire knowledge and training. In order to learn new ways of doing things, the employees must fully understand the current operation of the organization. Employees and leaders have to be able to answer these seven questions: (1) What is currently happening in the organization?

(2) How can this change improve what is currently happening? (3) How will this change impact the organization? (4) What would happen if we did nothing? (5) What are the obstructions or obstacles to implementing the change? (6) How could we implement this change? (7) Who will develop the plan and strategies for implementation? These questions require thought, collaboration and time to answer. They create opportunities for buy-in, partnership, and ownership.

When a leader attempts to define an organization and its operations, he/she must be certain they have thorough knowledge of the organization in its entirety. The question is does the leader really know the organization? The wise leader seeks various views and input on the identity of the organization and its operations. Looking from the top down is not enough. Looking from the bottom up is not enough. The leader must look at the organization as a whole. There are several activities and tactics available to ascertain enough data to define the organization and its operations. Some common ones are surveys, study groups, discussion groups, chat circles, suggestion boxes, outside consultants and surveyors. The leader must have an expansive view of defining the organization and its operations.

Paul Hersey and Kenneth H. Blanchard's book Management of Organizational Behavior: Utilizing Human Resources said, "Any change effort begins with the identification of problem(s). A problem in a situation exists when there is a discrepancy between what is actually happening (the real) and what you or someone who hired you (point of view) would like to be happening (the ideal)…change efforts involve attempting to reduce discrepancies between the real (actual) and the ideal."[1]

Moving the organization from the real toward the ideal is the task of the leader. However, a wise leader will share the authority for making it happen. It takes more than one set of eyes to fully identify and make an analysis of the problem. Once the problem or change is identified, the leader must seek out the cause or causes of the problem. These causes should be identified by people as close to the situation as possible. Sometimes people might be too close to "see the forest for the trees," but leaders have to seek involvement of people as close to the problem as possible. The cause of the problem could be the "system" or a general cause, such as the style of a supervisor, or co-workers. Once the problem has been identified and the causes defined, a plan of change can be created and implemented. All of these steps allow others to be involved in the problem solving and change process. A wise leader will utilize these opportunities to engage, involve and share ownership with followers or employees.

Kurt Lewin developed a process that leaders could use to ascertain the forces for and against a change. This process was called a "Force Field Analysis." Leaders should be aware of the forces in the company, organization, market, or community that are in favor of a proposed change (driving forces) and those who oppose the change (restraining forces).[2] It is a simple process to use. A leader can draw a horizontal line on a sheet of paper and place a vertical scale on the end of the line at point "0." Above the line on the scale, mark off five equal points of negative numbers. Below the line and the "0" point, mark off five equal positive points:

```
                                        -   5

                                        -   4

                                        -   3

                                        -   2

                                        -   1

                                            0

                                        +   1

                                        +   2

                                        +   3

                                        +   4

                                        +   5
```

The leader can now list in vertical columns all of the persons and groups supporting the change on the plus (+) side of the horizontal line and all the persons and groups opposed to the change above the horizontal line on the negative side (-). These pluses and minuses are forces for or against change. The items listed above the horizontal would be considered restraining forces and those below driving forces.

Some active parents become very concerned about the obesity of children in their school. They meet with the school superintendent and demand that all vending machines be removed from the schools. These parents assert that children are buying beverages, candy and other snacks loaded with sugar, fats and other non-nutritional ingredients from these vending machines. Two of the five school board members strongly support the parents' request. The high school, middle school and elementary principals oppose the request. These principals support keeping the machines, but changing the products being sold from them. The teachers are divided about supporting the request. The chamber of commerce is against removing the vending machines because they thought removing the machines would-be construed as anti-business. The students oppose the idea of removing the machines for obvious reasons.

The forces for the change and against the change in this example are fairly easy to identify. The field would look like this:

Forces against Change

(Restraining Forces)		− 5
Non Committed	School	− 4
Board Members	Principals	
Students		− 3
Chamber		− 2
		0
		+ 1
Forces for Change		+ 2
		+ 3
		+ 4
Two School	Some Parents	+ 5
Board Members	on a Mission	

(Driving Forces)

The superintendent can get a visual illustration of the forces for and against the proposed change by using the force field analysis process. This process allows the leader to examine the scope of the situation. At first glance, the leader could conclude that the forces against the change are greater than the forces for the change. But making this kind of decision is not that simple. Some forces are stronger than other forces. The superintendent is one vote away from having a majority of the board members in favor of the change. The leader must ascertain just how solid the board's position is on this matter. The active group of parents seems to be small now, but the leader must determine if this group is working to get the Parent-Teacher Organization to join them. In that case, the leader needs to determine the position of this organization. Engaging in this process is another means of involving more people in the change process. The solid compromise for this change is to keep the vending machines and change the food and beverage products within them.

How Effective Change Works

Leaders who want change to be successful and effective have to understand the power of getting followers to participate in the change process. In order for followers to participate in the change, several steps are necessary:

1.   Knowledge about the change has to be shared with the followers.
2.   Once followers have a positive attitude about the change, they are ready to make the change happen.

3.   Followers can help others understand and accept the change if they are given the appropriate opportunities to do so.

Involving followers in the process of change (participative change) is slower and more time consuming than issuing an administrative order (directive change). Top down directive change mandates are quick and less time consuming. These kinds of mandates are also "cold," impersonal, forced, and totally owned by the leader. These directive changes are imposed on the total organization and spread throughout the organization. In any organization there is a place for both kinds of change. Sometimes the leader does not have the luxury of the time needed for participative change. At other times, the situation will allow the leader the time needed to utilize the participative change method. However, changes resulting from the participation of all parties involved in the change seem to be longer lasting with greater ownership by followers. The downside of this kind of change is it is slower. Directive change is faster, but it can be volatile and divisive. Directive change has more risk of creating animosity and undercurrents of discord.

Communication

Leaders have to exercise good judgment in choosing which method of change to utilize because there will be opportunities to use both. Neither method will work effectively in every situation. Communication is a key part of any change. If change is occurring within the organization or the organization is being impacted by outside changes, communication is the key strategy for addressing it.

In preparing for change, the leader has to develop a plan that includes a comprehensive communication strategy. The participative change method will be slower and require a great deal of communication with followers. It seeks to involve a large number of people in the change development process and the need for timely communication is essential. The directive change method requires clear communication and guidelines because the leader wants everyone to understand what they have to do.

It would be wise for the leader to ascertain the current communication methods and means being employed in the organization before the change. There might be a need to revamp, overhaul or replace the current system of communication. When new leaders take over organizations, they should assess the communication patterns and procedures in place. It is important to understand the organization's communication pattern because it is a part of the culture and routine. Before a new leader changes this pattern he/she must understand the real message the new pattern of communication will be sending.

Change is a very powerful force. It can impact organizational cultures, products, procedures, goals, operations and existence. The impact of change is too important to be left to chance. Leadership is built on the ability to change and improve the organization. The greatest change the leader makes is in the minds of the people who choose to follow. Change should not be an excuse to fail, but an opportunity to succeed.

The Rope Metaphor for Change

The leader has to effectively communicate the value of change to the followers. The leader's rope is the key connection between the leader, the followers and the realization of the goal. Leaders educate followers to understand that the vision/plan is necessary to achieve the goal, but it is subject to improvement. Followers take ownership of the leader's rope with their eyes open for change. Many factors will produce changes that the leader and followers will have to overcome. The rope connects the leader and followers in times of change. As a matter of fact, in times of change the rope provides the security the leader and followers need to stay focused. The strands of beliefs, values, passion, purpose, courage and vision make the rope strong enough to handle the uncertainty of change.

Summary

Leadership failure based upon the inability to successfully and effectively deal with change is very real. Successful leaders accept the opportunity of leading and embrace the challenges of change. Organizations that fail to change are doomed to failure. Change is one of the essential requirements for continued success and operation.

The most effective change is created by leaders and

followers collaborating and taking ownership in the change. This is commonly called participative change because it allows participation by followers who will be impacted by the change. It is a slower method of creating change, but it commonly results in greater ownership and relationships. Directive change is imposed on the whole group. It is fast and often results in reduced ownership and poorer relations. Leaders sometimes have to utilize both methods of change. The method of change utilized depends on the leadership situation.

Communication is essential in the change process. A communication strategy should be part of every change plan. Leaders are wise to ascertain the forces for and against a proposed change before making the decision. One process for defining the restraining forces against change and the driving forces for the change is to use a "Force Field Analysis." This process was developed by Kurt Lewin and allows leaders to get a good look at the change proposal.

Change works best when followers: (1) have knowledge about the change and how it will impact them (2) followers buy into the plan and take action to involve others (3) followers change the attitude of others by sharing information and involving others in the problem solving activities (4) followers accept the change and develop ownership in it. These are steps in the participative change method.

Change is life and life dictates change. Leaders have to use change to lead more successfully and more effectively.

References:
1. Blanchard, K. H. & Hersey, P. (1977, 1972, 1969). Management of organizational behavior. Englewood Cliffs, New Jersey: Prentice Hall, Inc.
2. Lewin, K. (1951). Field theory in social science. New York, N.Y.: Harper & Brothers.

CHAPTER ELEVEN

FINAL THOUGHTS

FINAL THOUGHTS

This book is one man's thoughts gained from many leaders and leadership experiences over the past several years. To say this author has all the answers is far from the truth, but years of experience brings the multitude of thoughts shared with the readers.

The courage to hold on to one's rope is a tough task when the storms of leadership crash on the shores of life with the force of a hurricane focusing its onslaught of high winds and heavy rains on some awaiting landmass. The successful leader must make sure his/her feet are planted on the solid ground of principles and values and hold solidly to the rope so that those they are leading will likewise feel comfortable embracing the leader's vision.

Many excuses of leaders and the organizations they lead are given and used to try to soften the harsh winds of failure. These excuses are as weak as the sandbags that are sometimes used to try and hold off waters from overflowing streams and rivers. Just like the sandbags, the excuses may be a short term solution for failing to lead effectively, but also just like the sandbags, they cannot hold back the impending flood of failure in leadership. Effective leaders don't use excuses, they plan and implement change in organizations and in their own leadership to insure success in spite of rising troubled waters.

The rope metaphor has only been simplistically addressed in the pages of this book. As one might imagine it can be taken as far as the imagination will allow. Feel free to expand and adapt as you see fit. Such things as looking at the environment from the metaphor perspective may help leaders and future leaders to understand what they must do to succeed. If the environment is sunny and pleasant it is easy to lead successfully, but when those storms hit, the rope must be strong to withstand these changes.

If the reader is new to leadership he/she may feel they are just beginning to construct their rope or they have it constructed, but they are the only ones holding on to it. The leader's job is to get all the stakeholders eagerly and solidly holding on to the rope as well. At the beginning, the leader may get these followers holding, but they feel they are over the side of a cliff and clutching on the rope for their professional lives. The role of the leader is to "pull" and persuade these followers to come over the side of the cliff and finally walk down the road of success with leader and follower carrying a strong, successful, useful rope together for the good of the members of the organization and the organization itself.

The leader must be sure to continue to examine the length(s) of rope, the strands of the rope, and who is or is not holding on to it. Leadership is a continuous and complicated process. It is also a highly rewarding process both monetarily as well as intrinsically. Enjoy your leadership journey and be sure as you are walking down life's road of leadership to constantly look behind and in front of you to see that others have purchased your rope and are walking with you.